CUT THAT GRASS AND MAKE THAT CASH

HOW TO START
AND GROW A SUCCESSFUL
LAWN CARE AND
LANDSCAPING BUSINESS

PAUL JAMISON

Cut That Grass And Make That Cash

Paul Jamison

Copyright © 2021 Paul Jamison

ISBN: 978-0-578-83745-1

www.greenindustrypodcast.com

Dedication

*I would like to dedicate this book to the listeners of the
Green Industry Podcast. You guys are the best. I am thankful
for our community and that we challenge and encourage
one another to pursue greatness in our businesses.*

CONTENTS

INTRODUCTION

If you invested in a business book like this odds are you are a real go-getter, someone who goes the extra mile, and is high-powered. You have also likely discovered there are many great money-making opportunities in the Green Industry. As someone in my second decade in the industry I realize that is true, but also understand there are a lot of difficult challenges that if not properly navigated can lead to costly mistakes. These miscalculations and blunders can put us out of business in a hurry. My target in this book is by sharing my story, hopefully it will help you on your business journey avoid the mistakes I made and enjoy the benefits of what I learned to be the secrets to building a successful lawn care and landscaping business.

Our strong work ethic can not out earn our stupidity. Trust me, I tried. This book is full of entertaining stories explaining the lessons I learned through the school of experience. As host of the Green Industry Podcast I am often asked to share my business origin story and explain how I obtain customers such as the Head Coach and captain of the Atlanta Falcons. My reply is usually, how much time do you have? The reason being, this was not an overnight success story. It was actually a decade in the making with the scars and wounds to remind me of the hardship throughout the journey. Thankfully, I learned some valuable lessons with each misstep and look forward to sharing them with you.

1

I HAD AN IDEA!

In 2011 I was nearly clueless in life. I was a recent college graduate. I was deeply in debt with my student loans, credit cards, and I had a very low paying job. Statistically, I was living well below the poverty level. Thankfully, a friend of mine had turned me on to a fellow named Dave Ramsey. He had given me a CD (compact disc) series from Dave Ramsey called *Financial Peace University*. As I listened to the teachings and took notes along the way I realized I had a huge issue. My income was less than my expenses and I had dug a huge pit of debt but I only had a small shovel (income) to fill it in. The solution was obvious, get to work. I needed to earn more money, and fast.

To make matters worse, I had recently made a commitment that was very unwise. My buddy had just struck a deal with Randy Jackson from *American Idol* and was headed out west to pursue his music career. He asked me if I could stay at his home for a year and take care of the mortgage and utilities for twelve months. He said I could have roommates that could help pay the bills. At the time I was searching for a place to stay so I said yes. The problem was initially I could not find any roommates. So I was stuck with a $928 house payment each month, plus utilities. I begin to get paralyzed with fear and anxiety about money. How was I going to pay for all the bills I had? I was eagerly exploring several options of places to potentially work. And so one evening, I decided to truly take it to the Lord in prayer. I went on a "prayer walk" around the neighborhood. Perhaps my neighbors thought I was crazy, why was this guy talking to himself and walking? But, I was desperate, I needed money, I needed a miracle, I needed a breakthrough, I began to pour out my heart to God. I truly was casting my cares and anxieties upon Him asking for wisdom and a plan of what to do to be able to pay these bills. As I was walking, I arrived at a cul de sac and noticed something that caught my attention because it did not make any sense.

What was so strange and puzzling to me is there was a house "For Sale" but it looked like the grass had not been cut all year. It was like a forest. Overgrown grass, weeds up to my knees. I thought to myself what kind of Real Estate agent is this? Would it not make sense to have curb appeal? Make the place look nice? Who would roll up on this house and want to buy it when it looked abandoned? Out of curiosity, I called the number on the For Sale sign. A lady immediately answered. I introduced myself and told her my concern about this property. Not only was it an eyesore for our neighborhood but why would they let it get this overgrown if their goal is to sell it? The real estate agent explained to me that the gentleman who had maintained their listings for the last 20+ years was in the hospital and the timetable of his recovery kept getting expanded. Long story short, it was supposed to be attended to and they were giving time to their lawn guy to get it taken care of. But, because of his health situation, it had not been taken care of. What happened next changed my life forever.

Sometimes God delays his answers for our prayers, but sometimes there's a sudden answer. My motive in calling the real estate agent about this overgrown property is because it seemed unusual and I was just curious what the story was. But something wild happened. The real estate agent for whatever reason assumed I was a Lawn Care Professional. And so she asked me what my rate was to mow the grass and get the property up to par. As she asked me that question I felt like time literally froze and I was perhaps in a cartoon and the light bulb went off. The idea struck me, I can use the mower in my friend's garage, cut the grass, and make some cash? My emotions literally dramatically changed from fear and oppression to excitement and joy. Here I was literally on a prayer walk crying out to God for some provision and now a lady is offering to pay me to mow some grass.

What happened next was bittersweet. After a long pause, the real estate agent asked me again, "Just let me know the price and when you can get it done, and we will cut you a check. It should arrive in 2-3 business days." My long pause was because I was thinking, what in the world do I charge? I remember in high school I would cut my neighbor Frank's yard for $20. This property, however, looked like a forest. I figured I would probably have to mow it three times just to get the height of the turf to a reasonable height. In fear that she was going to hang up on me for my delayed response, I blurted out, $60 dollars. She said deal. She also told me if this gentleman was not able to get back to work immediately that she would have other properties for me to maintain as well. She gave me her email address and told me upon completion of the maintenance to email her and she would get the check in the mail. I would later learn what "check in the mail" really meant but will save that for a later chapter about billing best practices.

2

THEY DON'T CALL US ROOKIES FOR NOTHING

It truly took me near a decade to really understand that the dollars are in the data. That "knowing your numbers" or "being intimate" with your numbers is certainly vital to building a lasting successful business. Unfortunately, I completed countless jobs at a net loss. Eventually, I hit rock bottom and learned my lesson. I learned to truly calculate the finest details and to price jobs in a way to ensure they are profitable. But, that did not happen until more recently. And it certainly was not the norm in year one.

Right out of the gate my first job was in the red. I charged the customer $60, but I actually spent $200 to get the job done. Financially it was a - $140 loss and that's not counting the three days it took me to complete the job. Let me explain.

A few minutes after chatting with the real estate agent, the sun set. I was fired up. I would have started cutting the grass then, but since it was too dark my plan was to get started first thing in the morning. Now, at the time what I had to work with and out of, was my friend's Murray 21-inch non-self-propelled mower he got from Walmart and the 1997 Honda Accord I was renting from my other friend.

I woke up early that next morning. I could smell that $60. I needed that $60. Rent was quickly approaching. The amount of $928 and I need to scrape together every penny I could, as fast as I could, not to mention all the other bills that were beginning to pile up. I was quickly learning that life in the "real world" was a lot more challenging than my college days at Ohio University.

My plan was to get the grass cut in a couple of hours, email the real estate agent the invoice and hopefully have my $60 check-in two days and also secure those "other" properties that she mentioned needing to be taken care of. So I folded up the raggedy Walmart lawn mower and put it into the trunk of the 1997 Accord and I was off to my first property.

Upon arrival, I realized perhaps the grass/weeds were too wet. But, nevertheless, I was full of ambition. I unloaded the non-self-propelled push mower, cranked it up, and quickly realized I had a big problem. The grass, well let's be honest, the weeds were so tall and the mower was so weak that the mower kept cutting off. I was determined to try to make it work, but after trying for about an hour and barely making any progress I realized this mower was not going to get the job done. An array of thoughts began to plague me. Do I call the lady back and tell her I am unable to do the job? Should I go rent a mower from Home Depot? Then, I remembered my buddy Dave owned a landscaping company. I knew he had recently purchased a nursery, but perhaps he still had some lawn equipment from his previous business. And so I gave him a call to tell him about my situation and see if he could be of any assistance.

Thankfully, Dave still had the equipment from his landscaping company. He told me he had professional power equipment such as a string trimmer, or as we called it in Georgia a "weed eater" and he also had a commercial blade edger, and a 36 and 48-inch commercial mower. Being the generous guy he is, Dave told me that I could borrow any piece of equipment I needed to get the job done. This was very kind of Dave, but then I realized my next issue. How would I tow the 36 or 48-inch commercial mower, all I had was the 97 Accord I was renting from my friend. I could sense Dave was really busy because it was the spring and his nursery customers needed his attention. He told me the equipment was available but it was on me to figure out how to transport it.

The light at the end of the tunnel that I saw when I first chatted with the Real Estate agent about this mowing opportunity is now growing dim. Perhaps I will never see the $60 check. There was no way I could call my friend to tell him I could not pay the $928 rent. There had to be a way I could legally make money and stay afloat. But, this idea of a lawn business was starting to seem like it was not going to work out. The reality was sinking in. The non-self-propelled Walmart mower couldn't get the job done and I didn't have an economical way to tow the 36 or 48-inch mower over to the property. Even if I did, I had not experienced operating one of those commercial mowers. My only experience was my dad's 21-inch push mower I used in high school and my friend's Walmart mower that I used a couple of times to mow his small weed-infested yard. The thought of trying to operate one of those 36 or 48-inch commercial mowers seemed intimidating and dangerous. Then, I had a thought. I knew I had a friend with a truck and some lawn experience. Maybe he could help?

I gave him a call and told him my situation about trying to earn some money to pay rent. Then, I explained about my friend offering to loan me his commercial mowers to get the job done, but I did not know how to operate them and did not have any way to tow them. I explained that if I could get this property cleaned up in a timely way then the real estate agent would likely connect me to several other properties. Being the compassionate fellow he is, he said he could help me out this one time. He explained his schedule was pretty full but he had the afternoon free and could swing by pick up the mower, and mow the property for me real quick, but I would need to take it from there with doing all string trimmer work. And because I was in a desperate situation he said he would do it for only $30. He wanted to make sure some of the $60 check went to me to help with rent.

And so my friend picked up the 36-inch commercial mower headed over to the property. Apparently, I did not accurately convey the forest that he was arriving upon. My friend who has cut grass before said that was about the worst he had seen a property before. And so he raised the deck to the highest setting and went over it twice. He was tight on time, and just doing me a favor so that's all he could offer to help. I gave him $30 cash and expressed my thankfulness for his willingness to help. But, the property still needed a lot of attention. There was a big area in the back he did not feel comfortable mowing because there were rocks mingled in and I did not have any insurance and so he did not want to fling a rock through the house so suggested I weed eat the backyard. And the front yard was still full of clumps.

Nevertheless, I was making some progress and a step closer to getting that $60 check and perhaps some more properties.

There was also another interesting development that happened that day. Earlier in the day before my buddy double cut the property for me, I had an interesting conversation at the gym. During a break during my workout, I was having small talk with some of the staff. One of the personal trainers, a lady named Jamie asked what I did for my career. Maybe I was a little presumptuous in my answer but I replied that I was starting a lawn care company. Her eyes widened a bit and she explained that she had a side hustle doing landscaping and her college-aged son had a bunch of commercial lawn equipment and that he did several properties when he was not in class. She mentioned if I ever needed any help to reach out to her son.

I don't want to beat the dead horse, but I want to make sure to communicate -- I was desperate. The fear I had of having to call my friend to notify I was short of the rent payment was a terrifying thought. And so I humbled myself and called Jamie's son immediately after I left the gym. His name is Tyler and he answered and I told him about my situation and he explained to me a little about his equipment set up and customers. We struck a deal, he said we could work together, split the revenue for the day 50/50, we could use his equipment if I would help line up some customers. I said deal. Now, this was on a Monday, and his day off from classes was Thursday. And so I had two days to line up some customers.

In a future chapter, I will explain why Dave Ramsey shares that the only ship that doesn't sail is a partnership. But, first, let's continue with my humble beginnings.

With only two days to line up some customers, I knew I had to get to work fast on blitzing my neighborhood with some marketing. I went to the local print shop and printed some business cards. Paul Jamison Lawn Care. That was the name on the business cards with a very cheesy pic of a guy on a lawnmower and my number and new business email address.

I felt like I was on a roller coaster. My emotions were fluctuating. Excitement, then fear. Mostly fear, but there was still enough flashes of hope that I could see this turning into enough money to pay my bills. That's when the plot thickened.

The real estate agent called. She was following up if we had finished cleaning up the house for sale. My heart sank in my chest. I was hoping she would not contact me and we would get the job finished on Thursday when Tyler could help me. Nevertheless, I gave her an honest update and told her we would finish the job on Thursday and I would send her the pics of the property upon completion. She sounded irritated but said ok.

And so I spent Tuesday evening and all day Wednesday walking through the neighborhood I lived in and the neighborhood across the street sharing my business card. If I saw someone out and about I would personally hand them one and tell them who I was and how I would love the opportunity to mow their grass. If they were not home I would put my business card on their front door or position it on the outside of their mailbox. I literally passed out hundreds of business cards and to my surprise was landing some jobs.

I was able to intercept my neighbor Maria as she was getting out her brand new black Cadillac Escalade and asked if she needed her grass cut. She asked me for the price. I briefly looked at her yard and told her $25. She asked when I could do the maintenance and I told her Thursday. She said to sign her up for bi-weekly. Now, at the time I did not know that bi-weekly mowing in the Atlanta market was frowned upon. But, I was truly a rookie and was learning the hard way. As for the $25 rate to cut her grass. That was way off. Today I would likely charge at least $75 for that property. But, again I did not know what I was doing, I was just trying to earn some money to pay the rent and pay my bills.

In addition to Maria, I was able to sign up two more customers on Wednesday scheduled for Thursday's service. A gentleman named Reggie called me. He lived in my neighborhood and so I walked over and looked at his house. It was a super small yard and I told him $20. He explained that he had two big dogs and so I would need to coordinate with him what time we were arriving on Thursday so he could let the dogs inside upon our arrival. Another rookie mistake, I did not actually scan the backyard to notice all the holes back there from the dogs, and as you can guess by now the $20 rate was way below market value. I honestly had no idea that back in 2011 the Atlanta lawn care market was averaging about $45 per man hour, But, at the time I still had an employee mindset and so I figured $10 an hour. If it took 2 hours, $20. Obviously, I did not yet learn to calculate overhead, have any clue what the market was paying, and I did not know my worth. And so my prices were way too low. If you listen to my current podcast, the Green Industry Podcast, and hear us poking fun at "Rick's Mowing" or "Chuck in the Truck" it is all in good fun because that truly used to be me.

In my mind, on that Wednesday afternoon, the momentum

was building. I had lined up for Thursday the real estate agent's property grossing $60, Maria's yard for $25, and Reggie with the dogs for $20. Then, my phone rang again. Mrs. Stewart called me from the neighborhood across the street. I quickly drove over and looked at her yard. She explained to me in addition to mowing the grass, edging the borders, she would like for us to weed eat this huge slope in her backyard. I told her we would take care of it and quoted her $30. She said she would be at work during the day on Thursday when we came, but she would leave the check under the mat. Now, stay tuned in a later chapter, I will share billing best practices and the lessons learned about how to professionally collect payment in a timely manner. But, in year one I was figuring it out on the fly. Checks would later come in the mail (or not), under the mat, in the grill, hand me cash, or in some cases just not pay. As I said, I was learning my lessons the hard way.

The good news was, by the time Tyler called me on Wednesday evening to confirm our plan to work Thursday I was able to report I lined up four jobs for us. The real estate agent for $60, Maria for $25, Reggie for $20, and Mrs. Stewart for $30. That was $135 in revenue. Tyler had a couple of yards lined up for us too that were $45 each. So at the end of the day, we would earn $225, each making $112.50. Now, as you hear these numbers you are probably thinking that is pathetic, laughable, and underachieving. But, at the moment it sounded like success to me, My job in high school at Best Burger paid $7.15 an hour and in college, at the dining hall I was earning $8.50 plus a free lunch. Yes, there is such a thing as a free lunch. And so the thought of making over $100 in a day was exciting.

Wednesday night after confirming my plans with Tyler to get started at 9:00 am in the morning I drove over to my buddy Dave's house to pick up some of his equipment. Tyler said we could use his equipment too, but I wanted to bring some along as well. So Dave lent me his Stihl blade edger and string trimmer and little handheld blower.

Since I had never met Tyler before I was a little nervous. What if he didn't show up in the morning? What if he made fun of me for working too slow or not knowing what I am doing? That night I remember tossing and turning in bed, thinking what am I getting myself into. The roller coaster of emotions continued as this entrepreneurial journey began.

3

EYE OPENING FIRST SUMMER IN BUSINESS

I woke up Thursday morning to a picture-perfect Georgia spring day. The birds were chirping, the weather was beautiful, sunny, low 80s. Tyler pulled up in his white Chevy truck, open trailer right on time at 9:00 am. I introduced myself, hopped in the passenger seat and we drove across the neighborhood to get started on the real estate agent's house. It was a lot of weed eating in the backyard. Thankfully, we got the property cleaned up in a timely manner and then successfully banged out the rest of the properties and split the revenue to the day.

I was getting pumped up. As soon as I got home, before I showered and cleaned myself up I sent the invoice and pictures via email to the real estate agent. I was ready to get that $60 check. I realized I had lost money on that job, but I was still hopeful the real estate agent would hire me to do more of their properties.

To my surprise, the phone started ringing. People in my

neighborhood and the neighborhood across the street started following up and inquiring about my lawn care services. I was like Johnny on the spot whipping over to their property in the 97 Accord to give a quote. Then, on Saturday I got a huge breakthrough.

My friend Dr. Kim invited me to a cookout at his 1.25 million dollar beautiful home in St Ives Country Club in Atlanta. His home had a beautiful pool in the backyard and was on the golf course. I was telling him and his wife about my new business. His wife was explaining to me about their negative experience with their current lawn care provider and asked me if I would be interested in taking over their weekly maintenance. She told me they were paying him $45 per service. Thankfully, she had told me that information, because I would have probably done it for $25, so I told her absolutely. I can do it for $45 per maintenance. And, then their friend who lived in a nearby neighborhood asked if I could do their home while I was in the area. I said for sure! She told me they were paying $40 per maintenance and would love to hire me to help me get my business off the ground.

Business was booming! I did not have a truck, nor a trailer, nor any equipment. However, I was quickly assembling a lot of customers. That is when the real estate agent called me and asked me if I could maintain another listing she had until it sold! I swiftly replied YES! The momentum was building and my level of hope was rising.

4

A SAFE, LASTING SOLUTION

I have heard it said that the LORD is never late. His timing is different than ours because His perspective is radically different than ours. Well, this next story I will share is a testimony of that. The absolute perfect timing of this conversation I am about to share had a monumentally positive effect on my business and several of the key relationships in my life.

In the summer of 2010, I had a series of conversations with my roommate Chris about personal finance. He had studied finance at the University of Georgia and had seemed to be winning with money for someone who was in their early 20s. He was 100% debt-free, a pile of money in savings, and his income was substantially larger than mine and constantly seemed to be increasing. My situation at the time was the opposite. I had student loan debt, no savings, and my income was below the poverty level. And so I was all ears when Chris began to share his thoughts with me about money. Chris was very generous with his time as we would sit at the kitchen table and he would draw graphs and walk me through spreadsheets and try to explain to me his financial plan. He consistently mentioned Dave Ramsey's Financial Peace University class he had been through. At the moment the class was not in session, but he did give me the CD's he received in the class and the workbook that I could fill in the blanks as I listened to the CD series. Additionally, Chris suggested that I reach out to the gentleman named Kenny who taught the Dave Ramsey class at his local church. He explained that this fellow had a deep passion to help people transform their finances and that he would possibly meet with me one on one to help guide me through my oppressive situation. So Chris shared with me Kenny's cell phone number.

I called the coordinator of the Dave Ramsey class but he did not answer. And so I left a voicemail explaining who I was and that I was in much need of some help with my financial situation. I eagerly awaited a return phone call or text but never received one. Day after day, week after week I continued to wait. Then it turned into month after month and no reply. Perhaps he did not ever receive my message. Or maybe he did but is just too busy, I was overthinking things, but bottom line he never returned my call and voicemail.

Fast forward a year later. Now, it is the late spring of 2011. I am in the beginning stages of this new lawn care business. My customer list is growing daily and I was riding the wave of my first "spring rush". I was still borrowing my friend Dave's equipment when working solo and each Thursday I would team up with my friend Tyler. We would continue to predominately use his truck, trailer, and equipment and I would provide the majority of customers for that day and then we would just split the revenue 50/50. But, this is where things got dangerous.

Dave Ramsey shares that the only ship that does not sail is a partnership. I know that now, but I did not know that in 2011. As my passion for this lawn care business was growing so was my desire to be above board. The YouTube lawn care community that we know of today was not yet assembled back then, but there was still plenty of information on starting a business out there on the world wide web. I quickly realized that I needed to get a business license and get this lawn care business legitimate and professional as soon as possible.

After much research, I took a trip over to the offices of Gwinnett County to inquire about a business license. They gave me a packet of papers to fill out instructions on the next steps to get this business officially licensed through the county and state of Georgia. I was getting pumped. Once I had this paperwork processed and authorized I could go to the bank and get an official business checking account and have customers cut the check to the business instead of me.

As I began to look through the paperwork I came to a fork in the road. I needed to fill out what type of business this lawn care business was. There was an option for a sole proprietorship but also an option for a partnership. Without having a truck, trailer, and not one piece of equipment yet I was in a pinch. My buddy Tyler had the truck, open trailer, and commercial equipment and he was able to enter into his summer vacation from school and would have a lot more availability to work more frequently. And so I was leaning on signing up for a partnership. It made a lot of sense. I would continue to drive around in the rusty 97 Accord and do some guerilla marketing and then we can continue to use

Tyler's equipment and just split the money. And so I filled out the packet of paper from the county and the only piece of information needed to complete the paperwork was Tyler's signature. I was planning the next time we worked together he could sign it and then I would head over to the county offices and make this thing official. For the name of the business, I just kept it simple with his last name and my last name.

Now, back to that voicemail from last summer. Remember Kenny? The guy who never called me back when I reached out asking for help with my finances. I forgot to mention that he owned a landscaping company. And to my surprise, after about 1 year, one day, "out of the blue" he called me back. I had not saved his number so I answered thinking maybe it was a potential new lawn care customer calling and I was surprised when I answered and it was the man who taught the Dave Ramsey class. He opened up the conversation with a sincere apology for the delayed response and mentioned that he would be happy to meet me for a cup of coffee and will try his best to help me with my finances if I was still interested. Considering my financial situation at this point seemed to have gotten worse I immediately replied with a yes and so we schedule coffee for Wednesday at Panera Bread.

Believe it or not, back in 2011 I was not a coffee drinker yet and so I ordered a hot tea at Panera and had my pen ready and an open notebook as we sat outside on a beautiful spring day. Before we dove into the details about personal finance I shared with excitement about this budding lawn care business that was developing. Since Kenny owned a landscaping company I was not only interested in learning about money but I also wanted to pick his brain about the Green Industry. As I innocently shared about the last few months and all the twists and turns of this new lawn care business I could tell Kenny seemed uncomfortable and disturbed. His non-verbals were obvious but I kept sharing the origin story of my lawn care business. After I concluded bringing him up to speed he boldly and fiercely shared with me two gigantic mistakes that I made.

Have you ever been very excited about something just to have someone rain on your parade? I thought Kenny would have been thrilled about this opportunity for me and been celebrating what I thought was a success. But, he had great sobriety to his demeanor as he expressed his sincere concerns with me. He began by quoting Dave Ramsey. Considering that was the main reason for our meeting, it was fitting, but our conversation had not even visited the topic of paying off debt yet. Kenny quoted Ramsey, saying "The only ship that does not sail is a partnership." He said it again. Kenny asked if I had legally bound myself to this partnership yet? I shared that I had not, but I had all the paperwork filled out, it was sitting on my desk and just awaiting Tyler's signature, which I was planning on getting the next day.

In hindsight, this is one of those times I realized God is never late. What are the odds that I inquire with Kenny about meeting in the summer of 2010 and we don't actually end up meeting until nearly a year later on the day before I was about to legally sign into a partnership with my friend Tyler? Coincidence? I think not. Kenny, begin to explain multiple reasons why a partnership would not work. In his wisdom, he explained how Tyler and I could continue to work together throughout the summer in a way that is a win-win situation but how legally we should not bind ourselves together in a 50/50 partnership. Kenny emphasized at some point Tyler and myself would be in different stages of life and someone would be working with more diligence on the business and then whoever is not would get offended and then indubitable it would lead to conflict. He shared that my friendship with Tyler is in great jeopardy if signed that business license with the county.

Thankfully, Kenny intercepted me just in time from potentially ruining that relationship. Since that meeting with Kenny has occurred, my friendship with Tyler and his family has blossomed to the point that I would consider his family, family. I actually even lived in their home for a couple of years and they have helped me out in life in so many ways. Since most of my family lives in Ohio, South Carolina, and Texas the past several years I have spent Thanksgiving with Tyler's family, and our relationships have been prosperous and healthy. I am so thankful to God and Kenny for protecting me from entering into that partnership. Maintaining healthy relationships with the people you respect is very important. At the time I did not really understand that the only ship that does not sail is a partnership. But, now I do and I am eternally grateful to God and Kenny for speaking the truth to me in love.

I went ahead and filed the paperwork with the county as a sole proprietorship. I was the owner of the company and Tyler was very understanding. I would go on to work 3-4 days a week solo and would team up with Tyler 1-2 days a week that summer but would pay him as a subcontractor. He was just viewing the lawn care opportunities as a side hustle for some summertime fun money, whereas I was viewing it as my full-time career. Tyler would eventually go on to a successful career in business and to this day Tyler, his parents, and siblings are some of my best friends. God is typically not early, but He is never late.

5

ALL YOU NEED IS ROUTE DENSITY

In retrospect, my conversation with Kenny that day was one of the most impactful two hours of my life. I was, unknowingly, on the verge of making some big mistakes in life and business. Thankfully, Kenny had the courage to identify those pitfalls and help guide me on a better path.

With excitement, I shared with Kenny about how my first lawn customer was the real estate agent. I then shared the progression of how the real estate agent's staff was constantly providing work for me. It started with the one house in the neighborhood I lived in, then they connected me with several of their other listings. I thought this was such a blessing that the jobs were flowing in. Kenny in his wisdom though warned me that this was a giant trap. Here I thought I was winning, but Kenny clearly explained to me why I was not.

At the time Kenny had been in the Green Industry for almost two decades. That was just about as long as I had been alive. Kenny explained how in the early days of his business he was like me. He was driving north and south on interstate 85 and all around the busy streets of the metro Atlanta area. He would go from one property in Buckhead then drive over an hour to maintain a large commercial property over an hour away in Braselton. Mixed with the irritation of congested Atlanta traffic Kenny explained window time to me. When you really add up the drive time, and the wasted hours employees sit in the truck driving from one property to another, it can become a money-sucking problem. The goal is to be earning the maximum amount possible per man per hour. But, that revenue is not being produced while sitting in Atlanta's infamous traffic. Kenny went on to share with me how he struck gold when he began to break into one of Atlanta's most prestigious neighborhoods. His crew would enter the gates of the neighborhood as soon as they were permitted and literally work all day there   in just one neighborhood. There was minimal traffic and very short commutes between properties. A lot of times they would just park the truck in a cul de sac and maintain 2-3 properties before loading up to the next property at a nearby street in the same neighborhood. He taught me how this dramatically boosted his profit margins and reduced his stress levels.

Kenny then challenged me to think long term. My problem was I was thinking short term. How do I pay rent next month? How do I scrape together money for my upcoming bills and keep some fuel in the ole Accord? But, Kenny pointed out that if I kept doing all this work for the real estate agent I would get stuck in the trap of driving all around Atlanta as the listings were all over the place. That is when Kenny wisely challenged me to select the area I want to work in, then narrow it down to a neighborhood or two and create my marketing plan to work in those neighborhoods.

6

A ONCE-IN-A-LIFETIME OPPORTUNITY

In all honesty, my conversation with Kenny stung at the moment. Going into that meeting I had my plans to form a business partnership with Tyler and continue to build my business around servicing the listings of the real estate agent. But, after that cup of tea and two-hour conversation, I realized I needed to set the boundary and be the sole proprietor and narrow down my target market to a route dense area. Although, I appreciated my friend letting me live in his home for the year he did. I quickly realized his neighborhood and the one across the street where I eventually had several properties were not the two neighborhoods I wanted to target as my route-dense area.

Now, I understood I could not be too picky at the moment. I was still in a desperate financial situation. Every penny was valuable and it was not time to leave anything on the table. But, thinking long term I knew I needed to transition away from having a lot of my eggs in the real estate agent's basket and I needed to move out of the two neighborhoods I was working in where I was living when I started. I say this as delicately as I know how that the area was not the best area in town. It was notoriously known for crime, and I was continuously having problems with my clientele. Kenny encouraged me to go where the money was. Thankfully, I had one lawn in the neighborhood where my buddy lived in the 1.25 million dollar home on the golf course and so my plan was to try to recruit some of his neighbors as customers and around that time is when I got a big breakthrough, some may even call it a miracle.

Later that summer, the family that I was "house sitting" for needed to move back. And so I moved across town to an apartment complex. That is when I met my neighbor Vick. One afternoon I pulled into my parking space and as I walked up to my apartment Vick intercepted me and asked if I could give him a hand helping him move a couch. It was one of those awkward moments, I wanted to say no, but I didn't have the courage to do so and so I put on a fake smile and said sure I'll help. Just a little context, in college I had a job where I would help students move in and I strongly disliked that job. Moving heavy furniture up and down flights of stairs was not fun. No matter how hard I tried not to, it seemed like I was constantly jamming my finger in some doorway and pulling some muscles I never even knew existed. Anyway, not that I do not like helping out my neighbor, I just have the wounding experience of helping people move as a job and the negative memories that come with that experience.

Nevertheless, things quickly got strange with Vick. For whatever reason when he asked me to help move a couch I thought he meant at our apartment complex. Maybe move it from one room in his apartment to another or from the bed of a truck up to his apartment, but that was not the case. After I told Vick I would help him he seemed happy and told me to hop in his vehicle. Now, it was not a white van, but it still seems like a super sketchy situation. I did not really know Vick that well other than briefly saying hello to him if we passed each other in the parking lot of the common areas at the apartment complex. I did know that he did not have a job, so I was curious how he was paying all his bills although I never dared to ask. And so my mind was rushing with all kinds of thoughts. Should I back out of this commitment? What if I do get in his vehicle. Are we really going to move a couch? Or is this a trap to sucker me into some dangerous situation? I was very curious and concerned and so I just bluntly asked Vick to explain more about what exactly he was asking me to do. Where are we going and whose couch are we moving and where are we moving it to?

Vick laughed, realizing it did sound like a potentially sketchy invitation. He explained, his sister lives in the country club across the street and that it would take about 5 minutes to get to her home, and that we would be moving the couch for her. Now, this caught my attention. I always wondered what it looked like in the country club across the street. I knew the head coach of the Atlanta Falcons lived in there, as well as the Quarterback Matt Ryan as well as many other rich and famous folks. I had seen an episode of MTV Cribs that featured a rapper's house from within this neighborhood so I was excited to see these "cribs" up close and in person. And so I hopped into Vick's raggedy old Toyota Corolla and we departed for his sisters, well hopefully that's really where he was taking me. I was still a little skeptical, but there was no turning back at this point.

So we pulled out of the apartment complex and across the street to this grand country club. At the time, I had no idea that this would be the foundation of my business for the next decade. I had no idea that one day the Atlanta Falcons Head Coach would be one of my lawn care customers as well as their team captain and many of these other rich and famous people.

We slowly pulled up to the entrance. The security guard walked out of his guardhouse and asked for Vicks ID. I do not have the best memory in the world, but for some reason, this experience seemed to be living out in slow motion. It was like I knew at the time for some reason this was a defining moment. I had an unusual awareness that something special was happening. And so the security guard handed Vick his driver's license back and the gate slowly opened. And just like that, we were in. I had driven by this neighborhood for years, but because its perimeter is covered with large trees you can't see much. But, here we were driving right down the main street. I was taking it all in. The beautiful golf holes along the water and the large homes. I thought to myself, I want to work in this neighborhood.

So we pulled up to Vick's sister's house. We walked in and he introduced me to his sister as she gave us instructions on where to move the couch. Vick's story stood true, but at this point, my emotions shifted from the concern about moving this couch to thinking how can I get my lawn care company established in this fine neighborhood. I remembered what Kenny taught me about route density. I had only been in this neighborhood for a few minutes but I was already setting a big goal to invade this community with my services. Perhaps, I lacked social etiquette, but as Vick and I carried the couch through the house and safely positioned it in the beautiful large family room I blurted something out. I asked the homeowner Vick's sister, who is your lawn care provider. She answered and then fired back, why do you ask? I told her that I owned a lawn care company and would love to give her a quote. She replied that she was interested in my inquiry because her contract with her current provider was expiring at the end of the month and that she would be open to receiving my bid. She also mentioned that she is a real estate agent and has several listings within the neighborhood. It was like Deja Vu. Another opportunity with a real estate agent. However, this time her listings are not stretched across Atlanta, but they are conveniently all within the gates of this luxurious neighborhood. And so she gave me her email address and told me to send over my bid.

Now, I was still in the phase of my business where I did not know my numbers and I did not really understand the prices of the market. I was still somewhat under the employee mindset. Meaning, I would think back on my days earning an hourly wage and somehow use that influence when putting together my prices. I really was clueless that at the time the market was easily paying $45 per man-hour. But, I was charging way less than that. Needless to say, I emailed Vick's sister my quote of $35 per maintenance. Honestly, to this day I do not know her genuine reaction. But, let's just say if I were to quote that property today it would be a minimum of $100 per service. My price was well below market average and unfortunately well below profitability. However, it was a bargain and Vick's sister replied and asked me to get started beginning the next month. Although my price "innocently" was too low at least it got me in this exclusive neighborhood. And later on in this book, I will explain how I used that opportunity to build the majority of my customer base over the next decade in this one locale. It certainly did not happen overnight or even in that first year, but as I will explain later things eventually snowballed into some very profitable opportunities.

1

A LITTLE BIT OF ADVERSITY

Sometimes it really does feel like when it rains it pours. If you have ever been in a situation where you feel like you are robbing Peter to pay Paul then you know the stress of life in those moments. When the pile of bills is accumulating and the amount of money you have is not enough to pay for everything. That is how I felt my first year when I started my lawn care business and it seemed like life just kept getting more and more difficult. As previously mentioned my housing situation took a twist when the family I was helping out by living in their home needed to come back to Atlanta ahead of schedule. This forced me to find a new place to live quickly. And that move was a pricey one when you calculate the security deposit, administration fees, and all other expenses associated with a move.

Thankfully, I was able to find an apartment complex available in a better part of town. But, then I got another punch in the gut. The family who was renting me the rusty 97 Honda Accord contacted me that they had a family emergency and needed me to return the car immediately. Now, that is a whole nother story for another day and if you listen to the Green Industry Podcast you will have probably heard me discuss that incident. Let's just say the 97 Accord smelled like a gas station when I returned it since I was running my business out of it. Thankfully, everything was eventually resolved, but it is a humorous story in hindsight.

Even though the 97 Accord was not the most efficient set up for operating a lawn care company, it was all I had. At only $150 a month, it was economical and if I angled the weed eater and blade edger the right way diagonally from the passenger seat to the back seat, I could make it fit. Then, the handheld blower I used could fit in the trunk with the 21-inch push mower that I eventually bought off craigslist for $125. But now, that was gone. All I owned was a 21-inch push mower. I had no vehicle, no trailer, and was still "borrowing" my friend Dave's equipment. Although, I was beginning to sense I had outstayed my welcome if you know what I mean. He originally was trying to help me out of a jam, but now I was using his equipment daily and putting it through wear and tear. I needed to start purchasing my own power equipment, vehicle, trailer, etc.. but at the end of each month, it seemed like I had no money. I would later discover, and we will break this down in-depth but my prices were too low. I was working my rear end off but had seemingly nothing to show for it.

So here I was, living in an apartment with no furniture and operating a lawn care business with no vehicle and barely any equipment. The financial stress was overwhelming but like Dave Ramsey says the best place to go when you are broke is to work.

8

MOTIVATED TO ACHIEVE

As I reflect on life I realize many mistakes have come when I made decisions out of fear. I was truly at the fork in the road in the early days of my lawn care business. Because my prices were way too low, even though I was working hard. Inefficiently, I was pushing that 21-inch mower all day, sweating my butt off, hustling, grinding, giving it all I had. However, financially I was not getting ahead, I was falling behind. My expenses were consistently higher than my income. I knew I needed to upgrade my lawn care setup and equipment but I did not have the money. It took the opportunity to cut every blade of grass I could just to make rent. My operation was grossly inefficient, lacking experience, and dramatically underpricing my services. Quitting was a consideration, but I genuinely loved working outdoors and the satisfaction of making a customer's property look nice. I could see great potential with my business, but at the moment the challenges were paralyzing.

As I began to chat with a close friend of mine at the time about my stressful life and failing lawn care business, he had some clear advice for me. Get a job! The reality was running the numbers is I was going to be evicted soon and potentially homeless. I kept insisting I could make the lawn care business thrive, but week after week as I would touch base with my friend the numbers were telling a different story. I was broke. It truly felt like there were holes in my pocket. And so my friend, who was essentially my "spiritual advisor" at the time strongly encouraged me to get a job, where the pay was more steady. His advice was when I was not working that job I could be out cutting that grass and making that cash, but because I was in such a desperate situation I needed a job, immediately.

I really wrestled with this decision. I wanted to do lawn care full time. I thought I could make it happen, but the fear of being homeless. The embarrassment of being evicted, led me to start the job search. Because I did not have a vehicle, I went out on a bicycle to the local businesses around my apartment complex and began filling out applications. I went to Hilton Garden Inn and filled out their application. They actually called me in for an interview later that week, but never ended up offering me a job, I also went into the Carrabba's and asked if they were hiring. The restaurant was closed during the day, but ironically when I knocked on the front door the manager answered. I saw that there were cars in the parking lot so I figured someone must be inside. The manager, Mark, gave me an application and I began to walk back to my bicycle. I was embarrassed to park my bike by the front door so I actually hid it around the corner. As I walked around the corner to get back on my bike a man flagged me down. It was actually the owner of the restaurant. I was so embarrassed because he saw me sitting on my bike, but never-theless, he started asking me a series of questions and essentially hired me on the spot!

Now, you may be wondering why this was such a mistake. I was broke, wouldn't getting a job to produce some income to be able to pay my bills and stay afloat be a wise decision? Perhaps, but in retrospect, if I would have focused all of that time and energy that I eventually gave to waiting tables at Carrabba's to build my business, I could have experienced a breakthrough in my business faster. If I could go back in time, I would have doubled down on my lawn care business with a singular focus and worked with outrageous grit to make it work instead of being torn between being a restaurant employee and a rookie lawn care professional.

9

AN EXCITING CHANGE OF PACE

Although I regret working at Carrabba's there were some benefits to that job. The money! I was able to earn enough waiting tables daily to be able to stay afloat and eventually save up the necessary funds to purchase a truck and my own power equipment. Until I was able to complete my set up, I continued to work with Tyler when he was available using his truck and equipment, splitting the day's revenue with him. And my buddy Joe, who had a truck would work with me when he was available and we would use my friend Dave's equipment. It was not the ideal circumstances, but I saw the light at the end of the tunnel and knew I could eventually build this into a profitable healthy business.

I worked my butt off this season. Lawn care during the day, and waiting tables at night. I also would preach on Sundays. I repeated this schedule week after week. And over the next couple of years, I was able to really build up my lawn care business. My route density was getting tight and the demand for my services was ever-increasing. This led to a defining moment in my business.

In one of the neighborhoods, I had 75% of the properties on a specific street. There were eight homes and six of them were my customers. And so on one hot summer day, I had those six properties scheduled as well as four others. Ten properties total and as usual I had my shift at Carrabba's that evening.

This particular Georgia summer day seemed hotter than normal. One of those days where the sweat is dripping off my face in the morning. I knew it was going to be a long day and we were going to have to hustle to get everything done before I had to go home shower and get ready for my shift at Carrabba's. My buddy, Joe was going to help work with us for a little bit in the morning. Joe is an older fellow, retired Navy Seal, but usually only works half days and my friend Tyler was scheduled to work a half-day with me as well but he had to end his workday a little early because of a commitment that evening.

In addition to our regular mow, edge, trim and blow maintenances that were scheduled for the day. A new customer who lived around the corner requested that we do a bush trimming for their property. In hindsight, I should have never scheduled this job for the same day as the other ten maintenances, but I was young, dumb, and overly ambitious and so I told them we would get it done. I knew this guy was a "big shot" millionaire, and this was the first time he had requested work from us, and so I figured I should be Johnny on the Spot and get the job done. He was wanting to have it done promptly because he had guests coming in for the weekend and so I overcommitted myself. So I appointed Joe to take care of the bush trimming job while Tyler and myself go bang out the ten maintenances. As I mentioned, it was a scorching hot Georgia day. And Joe, being a little older, and needing to give attention to some health issues he deals with, decided he needed to call it quits earlier than usual. He got the bushes trimmed, but stopped after that, leaving a gigantic mess behind. While Tyler and myself were out banging out the maintenances Joe called to apologize and notify me that he was unable to complete the cleanup. I, unfortunately, did not receive this message until it was too late.

With Tyler needing to get done earlier himself, he and I were hustling. We got as much done as we could before he had to take off and I finished up the rest. Then, I headed home for a brief shower and swapped out clothes to my Carrabba's outfit to get ready to go serve tables for the night. Yes, I was burning the candle at both ends, but being evicted was not an option. I was working so hard to try to get ahead. It was a busy evening at the restaurant as there was a concert that night at the nearby arena so we were slammed. I had noticed an unusual amount of calls on my cell phone but was not able to check the voicemails or reply to any of my lawn customers who were attempting to contact me. I remember thinking did something happen, but I was so in the weeds waiting on the tables I was not able to follow up.

Finally, after my shift, being exhausted at about 10:30 pm I began to go through the many voicemails. My heart stopped when I got Joe's voicemail that he did not finish the job. This had never happened before, Joe has one of the most diligent work ethics I had ever seen. And to his credit, he did call me immediately after he made the decision to stop working because of his health and the Georgia heat. I just missed his call and did not even realize it until I got off work that evening from Carrabbas. And so needless to say, the other voicemails were from my customers on that street where we do 75% of the properties. The "millionaire" who we were trying to impress was obviously furious. His animated voicemails were him chewing me out that a) we cut the bushes too low and b) we did not bother to clean up. Now granted, he did not know the whole story, but he had every right to be upset because I never communicated why Joe had to stop and our plan to clean up. He continued to remind me that his guests were coming in and that the clippings needed to be cleaned up asap. If that was the only issue, things would have been alright. However, word quickly spread amongst neighbors that we hacked down the bushes and left all the clippings. The gossip and misunderstandings started to arise, but as I started to listen through the voicemails one after the other I realized this was not good. The customers from that street were contacting me one by one to inform me my services were no longer needed.

I was crushed. I sat in the parking lot at Carrabba's late that night heartbroken. I was working so hard. It took me two years to accumulate 6 properties on that one street. It was route density at its finest and now they all fired me. I truly was devastated. My physical body was exhausted. I felt like I was going 100 mph through life and barely getting anywhere. Emotionally, I was disappointed and spiritually I was getting fatigued. Where did I go wrong? God, where are you? I'm trying my best to make this work and it seemed like everything was falling apart.

I did not sleep well that night. I woke up while it was still dark and arrived at the customer's property as the sun was rising first thing in the morning to start cleaning up all the clippings. That was an interesting morning. The customer's wife was still livid with us and it was awkward seeing my other former customers out on the street that day after they fired me.

That is when I slowly started to realize this was a blessing in disguise. I literally was in tears. A grown man out doing yard work crying. Up until that point, I did not have much attrition at all. Maybe that was because my prices were way too low or I would like to think it was because I was reliable and doing a good job. Nevertheless, I was in shock that all these people canned me so abruptly. I didn't even have the opportunity to explain to them the reality of the situation of Joe getting light-headed because of the Georgia heat and needing to stop working for the day. But, the truth was, my business was unorganized. I bit off more than I could chew and because I was working full time at Carrabba's I was not able to fully monitor my business.

That is when the thought really started to penetrate, what if I did not work at Carrabba's? I would have likely caught those voicemails. I could have swung by after finishing the maintenance and cleaned up the clippings myself and perhaps avoided losing all those customers all at once? And so long story short or as my friend Naylor Taliaferro says, short story long, the seeds really started to get planted in my mind that I needed an exit strategy from Carrabba's and clear up more space in my schedule to build this business the right way. Although I was unusually emotional that day I slowly started to realize this was a minor setback for a major comeback.

10

A STEP IN THE RIGHT DIRECTION

A short time after suffering this traumatizing attrition in my business I received a very interesting phone call. My friend Ray Haynes had called me out of the blue. Now, Ray was the General Manager at a popular radio station in Atlanta. I had met him about seven years earlier and we would run into each other occasionally, but mainly we were "Facebook friends". When I saw him call I thought maybe it was a pocket dial, I had no idea why he would randomly call me? Anyway, I answered and we began to talk. That's when he asked me if I would be interested in hosting a radio show. I remember kind of laughing when he asked me. "What do you mean?" I replied. You see I had zero experience in radio. It was not like I had applied for a radio gig job or anything like that. But, Ray went on to explain that they were starting a new overnight show and that they needed a deejay to man the studio and be the on-air personality from midnight to six am. He explained that he knew I had no experience, but he trusted my character and work ethic and that they would take the time to teach me the broadcasting basics. The pay was not the most alluring figure, but the job opportunity was very fascinating. The hours were overnights on the weekend.

I gave this opportunity some serious thought and prayer of course. I thought I could work at the radio station on the weekends and then work on my lawn care company during the week. This would get me out of waiting tables. I truly did not like working at Carrabba's. I just worked there for the money. So after some time of consideration, I responded to Ray and told him I'm in. And the rest is history as they say.

Hindsight is 20/20 and again perhaps it would have been wiser for me back then to transition from Carrabba's and only work on and in my lawn care business. But, because I did take the radio job, I eventually got trained and grew in the development of being a broadcaster. This would later help when I started the Green Industry Podcast. It was a merger of my experiences from building my lawn and landscape company with my skills as a broadcaster. Additionally, while working at the radio station I was able to develop friendships with key people in my life such as Mr. Producer. For those wondering, Mr. Producer is the producer of my podcast and a dear friend and mentor in my life.

One of the unique ways the radio gig transformed my life was that it provided an opportunity for me to further my education in the Green Industry. Let me explain. After starting my lawn business, I was constantly working "in" my business. Yes, month after month I was growing and learning through my experiences. However, the rigors of life continued to keep me busy and I had quickly fallen into the rat on the wheel trap. I was accumulating so much work, but because my prices were too low, I felt as if I was never able to get ahead.

A huge blessing of this new radio gig on the weekends doing the overnight shift was that I was introduced to the YouTube lawn care community. How it all worked was my on-air shift would begin at midnight and end at 6:00 am. Now, I did not talk for six hours straight. The routine was that they would play 3-4 songs then I would come on live for about 2-3 minutes and talk, then they would go back to another 3-4 songs. In reality, I was typically only talking live on the air for about 12-15 minutes an hour and the music was filling the other 45 minutes. So while I was not on the air, I had some "free time". I would, of course, need to keep an eye on the radio programming to make sure we were on air and I would use this time to write scripts for my future radio segments, but midnight to 6:00 am was a long time and there were limited options. I was required to man the studio and often in those times when I was off the air and the songs were playing I would begin to watch YouTube.

I honestly do not recall what I typed into the search engine or if the algorithm just knew me well enough to recommend lawn bros videos but somehow I started watching these YouTube videos from Geek To Freak Lawn Care aka Greg Chism. Here I was sitting in a studio deep into the midnight hours watching this fellow named Greg from Illinois mow grass with his 21-inch Troy Built mower then doing a voiceover. These videos were super entertaining, but also very educational. My business was very similar to Greg's and so I would watch, night after night. Shift after shift. It was like I was getting an education, for free, while watching YouTube.

Each weekend I honestly looked forward to coming to work

at the radio station. Yes, my body clock was exhausted. Yes, I would get scared sometimes being all alone in the studio and I would see in the security camera when some random car would pull onto the property. Yes, I enjoyed being on-air, developing that skill, and sharing meaningful content with my audience. But, possibly most of all, I looked forward to those overnight shifts because it was a time for me to truly learn, get educated, and really thoughtfully analyze my lawn care business.

The more videos I would watch from Greg, the more YouTube began to recommend other videos to me on the right-hand side of the screen. This was back in 2014 when YouTube would recommend to me the Lawn Care Rookie. Even though I was a few years into my business, I was still making rookie mistakes so I figured I would watch this guy whose name was Naylor Taliaferro and see if I could learn a thing or two from his lawn care journey. Then, the algorithm suggested a kid named B&B Lawn Care. It was Blake Albertson and I was one of his first subscribers and again would learn from him as he shared about the early stages of his business. The recommendations kept pouring in. I was hungry for more information and motivation. Before I found these YouTube videos I felt like I hit a plateau in my business. I felt at times like it was vanity. I was sick and tired of working so hard but feeling like I was not getting ahead. But, as I began to watch Greg Chism, Naylor Taliaferro, and Blake Albertson's videos it was like something sparked inside of me. I found a newfound passion for my business. I was not alone, there were other guys out there going through the same problems and struggles in their business as I was! These videos were so refreshing.

That is when I watched my first Keith Kalfas video. I remember watching this guy from Michigan walking around a job site griping and complaining about the exact things I was going through. Was this guy my twin? It was like the exact thoughts that I was having but struggling to express and understand Keith was so bluntly explaining. I was instantly hooked to his videos. Of course, I smashed that subscribe button and started watching more and that's when I got a shot of confidence. Keith started sharing more and more of his story. The eviction notices, the stories of working hard and barely getting by. But he was getting some breakthrough and growth in his business as he was finding his worth and ultimately raising his prices. As I watched these Keith Kalfas videos I realized if he can do it, I can do it. These videos from these various lawn care and landscaping professionals on YouTube were game-changers. They were openly talking about their prices. As I attentively listened, I was hungry to learn more. More about their pricing, more about their business operations, more about their lives.

It honestly just kept getting better and better. Next, videos start popping up of this guy named Stanley "Dirt Monkey" Genadek. I started watching him too. He would sit in his office and talk numbers and how to quote and do billing. I was hanging on every word. If I would have paid this much attention to my teachers in high school and college, I am sure I would have earned better grades. But, the truth was I was so desperate for this information and so I intently watched and listened and learned and learned and learned. I experienced such a renewal as a business owner.

Have you ever seen that candle that was just about to go out? I'm talking about when that flame is so weak and at any second is going to go out. Before, I started watching these YouTube videos from the lawn and landscape community that was describing me and my business. But, after viewing these videos weekend after weekend I got revitalized. It was like God blew on my weak flame and I was fired up. I was ready to turn the corner in my business. I was ready to be more professional. My confidence was growing to charge higher prices. And what was becoming work that I was beginning to despise was now becoming fun again.

There are many names of other YouTube creators that I watched in those days that helped influence my business as well. Jason Creel, Brian "Top Notch" Shain, Johnny Mow, Jonathan Potashanik, aka the Lawn Care Millionaire, and many others I would watch. I was not watching for entertainment or companionship, although some of their videos were very entertaining. And yes, it would get lonely working the graveyard shift alone, so these videos did have an element of companionship. But, what brought me back weekend after weekend was the business lessons I was learning that I was able to immediately implement in my lawn care business the next Monday. And what pumped me up was there was a real correlation between the results I was experiencing. My revenue and profit were truly growing and I know 100% it was because of the information I was receiving from watching these videos.

11

MY MENTORS FRESH PERSPECTIVE

I have already mentioned in this book Kenny. He truly was a huge blessing to me in the first couple of years of my business helping me avoid some traps and guide me into some industry best practices. Then, I was blessed as a viewer of YouTube videos and learning from other Green Industry professionals who shared their journeys and business advice on that platform. Now, I would like to share about a few more mentors that helped me take my business to the next level. In the book of Proverbs, it warns that pride goes before destruction. As go-getters, entrepreneurs, sometimes we can be stubborn and not want to reach out for help. However, when we humble ourselves and ask for help. From God and from those further along in life than us, it can have its many blessings. The following mentors I am going to share about were light years ahead of me in understanding the Green Industry. Rich had worked for some of the larger companies in the industry as well as owning his own business. And Jamie has also worked for one of the best local companies, has the top certifications, and also the experience of owning her own business. And so I humbled myself and asked for help.

Now, before I shared the transformational ways that both Rich and Jamie dramatically helped improve my business let me give a warning. Nobody likes a person who acts like a parasite. A leaching person is somebody who sponges off others. When a relationship is lopsided and somebody is always giving and the other is always taking, it can be very toxic and unhealthy. So to clarify, when I said I humbled myself and asked for help, this was never in a parasitic or leaching way. As I am going to share I was very blessed by both Rich and Jamie for taking the time to invest their knowledge into me and help guide me into deeper success in my business. As they blessed me though, I aggressively looked for ways to bless them as well. This would come in the way of offering my time to help maintain Jamie's beautiful 35 acres of land. I did what I could to mow and trim their property without being asked to. Or in the case of Rich referring some of my high-end customers to his lighting company, where he was able to do some high-ticket priced installation jobs and make a good profit. I say all that to emphasize, as mentors come along and help us take our businesses to the next level, may we be mindful not to ever become like a leach but rather that we would be grateful and keep the generosity flowing in whatever ways we may. With that disclaimer out of the way, it brings joy to my soul to share how Rich and Jamie positively influenced my business.

As a podcast host, I have now done hundreds of interviews with business leaders and I have noticed a particular phrase that successful people continue to share. If you are an avid listener of my show, you probably already know what that is. Know your numbers. Unfortunately, during my first several years in the business I didn't really have intimacy with my numbers. Now, I was not overly sloppy, I actually had multiple spreadsheets. One for my personal expenses, I was aware of what I needed to make to pay the basic household bills. I had a spreadsheet for my debt snowball, that listed my debts, the interest rates, and balance. I even had a detailed spreadsheet for my customer base. But, the truth was I did not really know my numbers. At the time I did not have a professional bookkeeper because I could not rationalize paying one. Money was so tight, it was like I was one of those jugglers at the circus. I was juggling all my bills. I was constantly stressing about money. I would be rushing through jobs to get it done so I could get the check just so I could pay a bill and the cycle seemed never-ending. I was trapped, I was stuck, but to those around me, I looked like I had it all together. Well, at least that is what Rich thought.

You see, I was working in one of the most prestigious communities in Atlanta. Many of my clients were famous and the majority of them were very wealthy. And so by the looks of things I must be doing pretty well. The reality though was my business was struggling. I was so busy with work, the next job, that I did not fully realize this. But, thankfully Rich had the relational intelligence to offer some help.

Initially, I think Rich thought I was a rock star. I mean I was working at mansions and my customers that I referred to Rich would speak very highly of the quality of our work. Rich noticed I was doing these ten and fifteen thousand dollar jobs one after another. But, then when Rich and myself would cross paths out in the field and get to talk I began to constantly ask Rich money questions. I was frequently picking his brain about pricing, paying off debt, and basic business operation finance. Thankfully, he realized I was struggling. He then invited me over for a steak dinner and told me if I could bring all my financials he could help me out. Honestly, I was a little nervous. Nobody, other than my accountant, saw behind the curtain of my numbers. I did not really know if he would look at my numbers, give me a high five and tell me to keep it up or if he would have another opinion, I did not exactly know, but I did know that I was stuck and needed help and so I accepted his invitation.

It was a Sunday evening. At this point, my radio show shifts had changed and I was only working at the radio station on Sunday afternoons. So after a long day "on-air" I was exhausted, but when I got to Rich's home that smell of a home-cooked steak dinner reenergized me. The aroma was sweet as his wife cooked a delicious meal.

Rich had requested I bring my bank statements, reports from Quickbooks, as well as the stats that I was collecting from how long the various jobs would take us. I had a pile of information that I laid before Rich. Now, he had worked for a couple of very large and reputable companies in the Green Industry earlier in his career. Not just out in the field, but in the office. He knew how these companies crunched their numbers, and what key performance indicators they were looking for. And so needless to say Rich got right to work with his pencil and calculator as he aggressively was analyzing my financial information. I just sat there for what felt like an eternity as he wore out the calculator and kept writing notes and that is when everything climaxed. Rich put his glasses at the end of his nose and dropped his pencil and stared at me. I literally felt my heart sink. It did not take too much intuition to sense from Rich's non-verbal communication that he was disturbed. He continued to stare at me then softly spoke, "How are you paying your bills?" Greatly embarrassed I hesitantly replied that things were tight. Rich responded with his amazement that he was surprised I was staying afloat and that he had no idea that things were this bad.

This was truly a defining moment in my life. It honestly felt like time froze. Rich slowly began to share his notes with me and explain why my business was a trainwreck. He went through customer by customer and showed me that I was averaging between $20-25 per man-hour. Thankfully, I had been logging throughout the past year what time we clocked into the property and what time we clocked out. So Rich then took the averages of the time we spent maintaining properties with how much we were getting paid to conclude that something was way off. The deeper he dug into the data the more clear it became that my prices were way too low and I lacked overall efficiency to complete our services. I was left with a couple of options. Either go get a job and use that income to start paying off my debt or if I was going to continue with my lawn and landscape business I was going to need to make some major changes immediately.

This was the night my rate increase letter was birthed. For those who are Green Industry Podcast listeners you likely know about my rate increase letter. This was a letter written to inform my customer that their rate was being adjusted. My issue though was that my price was so low, that I was literally going to need to double most of my customer prices. It was that bad. Accounts I was charging $225 a month, needed to be $400 a month or more.

I had started my lawn business to dig myself out of the pit I was in at the time, but now I realized I was in an even bigger pit. I had built all these relationships with my customers, I have all these commitments to service their property, but as Rich explained it was basically like I was paying them to work on their property. The numbers showed my business was losing money and the only thing that kept me afloat was my frugal lifestyle and the income I had from the radio station and Carrabba's.

Although this meeting with Rich felt like a punch in the gut. It was the wake-up call I needed. I was revitalized, refocused, and ready to increase my prices, efficiency, and profit. The momentum was swinging in my favor.

Rich's experience in the industry lit a fire in me to dial in on my numbers and simultaneously to this financial renaissance my friend Jamie was helping me with another area of my business. Jamie is Tyler's mother. Remember Tyler? My friend who helped out the first summer when my lawn business got started. Well, his mother Jamie, is a certified landscape professional who is very knowledgeable and skillful at doing landscaping.

Through an interesting series of events, I was presented with the opportunity to actually live with Jamie's big family at their large home. Jamie, her husband Derrick, and their family live on 35 beautiful acres, with lots of animals, and a beautiful large home. They had an extra bedroom and bathroom available and gave me a deal I could not refuse and so I was blessed to live with their family for a season.

There were many blessings living with this great family and one of those is that Jamie taught me so much about landscaping. Jamie and her husband Derrick have what I would call a spirit of excellence. Some may call them perfectionists. You can label it or name it however you would like, but the fact of the matter is they produce some of the finest work I have ever seen. Their landscape remodels are stunning as they consistently transform their clients' landscapes.

When I started my business in 2011 I had minimal experience and knowledge about lawn care and landscaping. I would eventually learn the ropes through everyday experience in the field. Conversation after conversation with peers in the field helped me learn a lot and of course those YouTube videos. But, everything expedited when I lived with Jamie's family. From going to classes with Jamie at the County Extension Offices, to real-life instruction out in the field, or sitting around the table while Jamie was architecturally designing drawings for her clients, I was continuing to learn about the actual practical how to's of landscape enhancements. From dimensions, to color schemes, to understanding what trees and plants perform best in various climate conditions I was learning day after day. Just like Rich had great relationship intelligence so did Jamie. She recognized I was eager to work and get after it, but I lacked some of the basic knowledge that professionals of her caliber had.

As previously mentioned, I was very self-aware not to be a leach. Jamie was constantly pouring out valuable information and knowledge that taught me the proper way to operate a land-scaping company. I may not have realized it at the exact moment, but I was becoming an expert. Jamie had the reputation from her clients and other peers in the industry that her company was the best of the best. The quality of their work was second to none. Her crew has such a passion for excellence. Making things look the best they possibly can. And that spirit of excellence began to rub off on me.

What was happening is that a solid foundation was beginning to be built in my business. Rich was continuing to keep me accountable to get my numbers right and boost my profitability while Jamie was teaching me the knowledge and skills to truly be a professional that can tackle specialized and larger jobs. With their help and guidance, my confidence was growing and new doors of opportunity were flinging wide open.

12

MAYBE IT IS TIME TO SAY NO

When I was in college at Ohio University I was a part of a student club called Cru and I was blessed to be invited to one of their summer leadership retreats. At the time I was only a sophomore and the majority of other attendees of this leadership retreat were juniors and seniors along with several Cru staff members. The leader of the bunch was a guy by the name of Brian McCollister. Brian was a very humble and wise man and I had a lot of respect for him and his impeccable character. And so I was attentively listening as he said he was about to give us the most important leadership advice that he had to offer. Brian emphasized that hot summer day in the foothills of the Appalachian mountains in Southeast Ohio that we needed to learn to say "NO." Brian explained that as leaders of the largest club on campus over the course of the school year we would be presented with many opportunities. He explained that there is tension and pressure to feel obligated to say yes and help out when called upon. But, Brian explained that we needed to say no. Once we start saying yes to too much, we overextend ourselves and we will quickly lose our effectiveness as leaders. As a college sophomore enjoying my summer vacation it sounded like wise words but it kind of went in one ear and out the other.

Fast forward a decade later however and I began to recall what Brian once taught me. "You need to learn to say no." As my influence in the community I worked in began to grow, as well as my knowledge about lawn care and landscaping, I felt like I was being bombarded at every side with opportunities. My wealthy clientele was consistently inviting me to go play golf at some of Atlanta's finest courses, I was invited on vacations, out to the lake, to baseball games, football games, and to dinner parties and social events. The invitations to socialize were pouring in and I was naively saying yes, yes, yes. Simultaneously to the social invitations, the job referrals were piling in. My marketing budget was slim because the word of mouth referrals from the community I worked in was keeping the pipeline full. We would be booked for weeks, but the job inquiries seemed to only increase. When somebody rolls up to a job site in their Lamborghini and asks you to swing by and give them a quote to repeat the exact same remodel you are currently doing for their yard-- it's hard to say no. And so I would drop what I am doing and go and take measurements and give out quotes. As the social opportunities and new jobs were piling up so were the fires. It seemed like as soon as I would solve one problem, something new would arise. Whether it was a busted pipe, flat tire, broken piece of equipment, or an employee quitting, it never seemed to stop. My business kept growing, but so was my stress and anxiety.

This is when another mentor of mine, named David Stein

challenged me with the skill of saying no. David would meet me for coffee and he had so much peace to his demeanor. Whereas I was overwhelmed, David seemed so calm. He read me like a book. He explained what he learned over the years of his seasoned life is that we need margin. Not just margin in our finances, but margin in our schedule. David was gentle in his delivery but very clear in his message. My schedule was too full. I bit off more than I could chew. And as David pointed out there was no slowing me down until I got the courage and self-control to say no.

Another memory I have from my college days at Ohio University was the song we would sing at the small Baptist church I attended on Sunday mornings. When I say a small church, I mean small. I was typically the only student there and there were a few older folks that attended. All in all, there were probably about 20-30 people in attendance on Sunday morning and so when we would sing, you could hear all those who were engaging. I say that tongue in cheek emphasizing it may not have been the best sounding singing ever, but I remember the rich lyrics of this one hymn we would sing called Take It To The Lord In Prayer.

And so that is what I started to do with my business and schedule. My mind was struggling, The majority of the opportunities presented to me seemed good. They were ways to earn revenue, build my business, and maintain my reputation as being "Johnny On The Spot" who is dependable and reliable. The deeper issue was simply that I did not have clear boundaries. David explained to me that it is important to first establish your priorities and what you want to say yes to. Once there is clarity with those priorities, then the boundaries can be established and there can be a more precision of when to say yes and when to say no.

13

A HEALTHFUL WAY TO TIME MANAGEMENT

Two main areas where I needed to establish better boundaries were with my schedule and health. I realized there was a correlation between the two. As my business grew I quickly fell into the trap of being overworked. The bills needed to be paid, and I needed to keep the money flowing in. And so I worked, and worked, and worked, and worked. 7 days a week. Keep in mind on Sundays I was working my radio job, but the other six days were also spent working. Now, I know "hustling" and "grinding" can be glamorized in this as entrepreneurship is the new sexy title. And I also understand that with proper diligence and work ethic can come great prosperity and success. But, I had crossed the line. My schedule was not balanced. I was so overworked that the work was not always done efficiently. I would make mistakes because of fatigue. Sometimes the mistake was in the field, but more often it was in the office assembling a bid, or lacking in prompt customer service. I would get so overwhelmed and overlook simple details that would be costly. I realized I needed to get in better control of my schedule and certainly do whatever it takes to improve my health.

To help with my out of control schedule I turned to some trusted friends. There is a group of three men in my life who keep me accountable in other areas of my life such as sexuality. Being pure in mind and heart and saving myself for marriage is a top priority. And thankfully these three men have been faithful to help me on that journey. And I realized if they could help me with clean living and making wise decisions with my boundaries with women, they should be able to help me with my schedule as well. And so that's exactly what I did. I shared my struggle of being overworked and running low on energy with these three men and asked them to help keep me accountable to make real changes.

Step one with my schedule was that I needed a designated day off. The Bible teaches the ratio of working six days and taking a day off. Yet, there I was working seven. I would start Monday morning at a disadvantage because I was already exhausted. Actually, I was tired on Sunday when performing my broadcasting duties. I was fatigued on Saturdays when I was out in the field. And truth be told I was running on fumes most of the week. It was a very bad cycle. I was operating on caffeine, too little sleep, and an overall lack of energy. The glory of young men is their strength. But I felt like my glory was in my tiredness and stress. But, with the accountability of my three friends and some intentional decision making, I decided no matter what--I was going to take one day a week and truly have an off day. A day to rejuvenate, rest, heal, refocus, and recover. At first, this was not easy, because I did not know how to push pause when there was work to be done. But, eventually, again with the help of my friends keeping me accountable, I was able to set this day aside and make it happen. What is interesting is that it did make a difference. Even though now I was only working six days a week, it felt like I was getting more accomplished in those six days than I was previously in seven. And not to mention it also had positive effects on my health. It kind of made sense to me as part of Chick-fil-a's success. They were open six days a week but off one. Yet, they seem to run circles around the competition. I was late to the game, but this was a valuable lesson I finally learned. It is of utmost importance to truly have a day off once a week to rest. I am all about working diligently on the days when it is time to get it done, but I now realize it is equally as important to have that day of rest and rejuvenation each week as well.

Now as I was gaining some victory with a more manageable schedule, I was still dealing with the battle with my health. One of the biggest challenges contractors face is that we can be in our trucks and out in the field most of the day. With that schedule and circumstances, it can be a big challenge to eat healthy and receive the proper amount of nutrition. As I sit down to write this book I am thankfully feeling healthy and weighing in at 180 pounds. But, that was not always the case.

There was a season when I did not have good boundaries in my business and you could say I let myself go. I gained a lot of weight, I packed on the lbs all the way up to 222 pounds. I was skinny my whole life, so this was a surprise to many people. But, it was not a surprise to me. On a regular workday, my breakfast would consist of a Dunkin Donuts coffee, two creams, two sugar, and either a stop through Chick-fil-a if the line was manageable or I would just stop at Panera. For lunch, it would typically be Wendy's, Chipotle, or Moe's as those were the nearest restaurants located next to the community we worked in. Then, after a long day, I would be hungry and typically stop by a drive-thru to pick something up on my drive home as I crawled through that frustrating Atlanta traffic. In summary, I would eat fast food three times a day. Not only was this financially stupid, but it was not being a good steward of the body that God has entrusted with me. In this season I was eating unhealthy foods and I was also not doing close to a regular, consistent, workout routine. There would be the rare and occasional day when I stopped by the gym for a workout, perhaps on a rainy day but it was never anything consistent. The main reason was not my schedule, although that was a factor. The main reason was my energy level was so low, I did not think I could power through a workout session and somehow have the energy to make it through the workday. At this point in my business, I was working in the field doing lawn maintenance and landscape enhancement. That line of work can be very strenuous, especially considering the hot summer days in Georgia.

This is where my friend David's advice helped again. Remember he said in order to know what to say no to you must first identify what you want to say yes to. I determined in my heart I wanted to say yes to vibrant health. I wanted to say yes to consistently going to the gym and working out again. Please don't laugh, but I wanted to say yes to having a flat stomach and perhaps even a six-pack again. I say again because in my high school days I had a six-pack. I remembered back to those high school days when it seemed I had all the time in the world. When I would spend hours at the local YMCA, playing basketball, working out. But, now that I owned this budding lawn and landscape company I did not have that kind of free time anymore. But, I did have those three friends who help keep me accountable for remaining pure sexually, and they have helped me set up boundaries with my schedule. And so I reached out and also asked if they would please keep me accountable on this journey to better health.

Now, you do not go from 222 lbs to 180 lbs overnight. But, the transformation started and was in progress when I clearly identified the goal to intentionally pursue better health. I was able to begin to say NO to certain restaurants and diet decisions and say yes to wiser healthier choices. I also started to discipline myself to go to bed earlier. If I was going to wake up early and get a good workout in, I needed a good night's rest. This meant turning off the TV, skipping out on watching Sunday Night, Monday Night, and Thursday Night football, and getting to bed. I realized if I was going to wake up at 5 or 5:30 am and have some energy I needed to get to bed on time.

In conclusion, this health journey continues. We reap what we sow. And I have radically changed what I have sown. To this day I continue to try to eat healthful foods, exercise consistently, stay hydrated, and get proper rest. I believe as entrepreneurs we need to be on top of our game. Strong focus and vibrant energy are important in making wise business decisions and so I am committed to keeping a high priority on a healthy lifestyle moving forward.

14

AN EXCITING NEW WAY TO EFFECTIVELY COMPLETE BILLING

I had heard the words delegate and automate many times when listening to a business podcast or audiobook. It sounded so elegant and wise, but it seemed challenging for me to actually implement into my lawn and landscape business. In my mind, nobody could lay down stripes like me. Nobody could meticulously edge a border around a garden bed like me. Nobody could edge a driveway and blow out the channel afterward like me. Nobody could grade and install sod as tightly and perfectly as me. The list goes on and on. But, that was my problem, I was trying to do everything myself and it was creating many problems. The transitions into automating and delegating were not necessarily the smoothest. I made some mistakes along the way, but choosing to get things in order by delegation and automation certainly was a wise decision and with technology and software ever-evolving it takes great intentionality to stay ahead of the curve. I made some decisions in the way I do billing that were so important and changed the trajectory of my business for the better.

A running joke on my podcast is the saying, "Checks in the mail." Perhaps some of the newer guys in the industry may not get it. Nowadays it's common for guys to start out day one and implement a CRM, Customer Relationship Management. But, back when I started my business collecting payments and communicating with customers was a whole different ball game. Utilizing software and technology to efficiently operate my business is something I wish I would have adopted much earlier. Unfortunately, this was one of those lessons learned the hard way. Nevertheless, this is what I learned.

Cash flow is vital. When there is a surplus, a healthy margin, I seemed to experience more peace and thus made wiser decisions. However, when I found myself obsessing with bank account balances and jumping through hoops to stay on top of my bills, I would experience a lot of stress. Looking back, I had the tendency to make poor decisions in those tense moments of stress and anxiety. In the next chapter, I will share about profitable pricing and how the dollars are in the data. Eliminating the stress and replacing it with peace had many components to it. The pricing needed to be at a profitable rate, the efficiency of getting the work done needed to be executed with precision. And also the billing needed to be conducted in a way to make sure I was paid promptly for the services we provided.

For a while, in the early days, I would gripe and complain about how inconsiderate some customers were. We would maintain their property all month, 4 or 5 services depending on the month, and then when I would attempt to collect a payment--a payment it seemed like they were conveniently missing. My bills were staring me down and as I was attempting to collect the money owed to me, it seemed like there was a constant delay and in some extreme cases even non-payment. I would complain to my friends and fellow business owners. The more I talked and aired my frustration, the more blame I would place on my customers. It was all their fault. Or was it?

This is when one of my mentors asked me a tough question. Is it really your customer's fault for the delayed payments? Well of course I thought and eventually responded. But, this was one of those rhetorical questions. The correct answer was actually it was my fault as the business owner. My company policies were not clearly defined and certainly not evidently clear to my customers. In trying to be a nice and reasonable guy, I muddied the waters. Failing to set clear expectations to my customers of when they were to pay, I clearly was not maximizing the advantages of the software and technology available to receive payments quickly and easily.

Realizing I was the problem was a huge breakthrough. Once I agreed with the reality that the man I see in the mirror each morning was the problem, then I was able to begin to step into some solutions that would truly transform my business.

Step one was establishing clear company policies and sticking to them no matter what. Prior to this, I was very flexible. Flexibility has its benefits in certain situations, but when it comes to billing, and making sure I am ahead of the game with cash flow, flexibility can be dangerous. As I began to implement and enforce my company's new billing policies something interesting happened. My bank accounts began to beef up, my stress levels began to reduce. I gained a natural poise and confidence when communicating my billing practices and payment expectations to customers and they also experienced comfort and received clarity.

Now, let's dive deep into these policies and how I utilized a CRM to get paid on time. The easy part was communicating with all new customers how and when they were to pay. From the point of my transition to this day that has been a rather seamless and easy transition. Customers like great communication, when things are simple and clear, it makes life a lot easier for them. I have heard it said, "To be unclear is to be unkind." Now I am crystal clear with new customers of how we do business. This communication is what people expect from a professional, and it is very clear, leaving no room for confusion or any gray areas. I will explain our company billing policies in a moment. First, let me address what was the challenge. This was converting my old customers to my new ways. The sloppy billing and poor foundations need to be dealt with and that process was a challenge. Because of my ignorance and immaturity, I essentially created customized payment plans with each individual customer. Some paid through PayPal, while others mailed me a check, others handed me cash, some left the check in the grill, under the mat, or taped to the front door. I was constantly sending out text messages, phone calls, leaving voicemails, and sending out emails in an attempt to collect money.

Overall, I would consider myself an organized person. If you would see my home, it is very orderly. Clutter irritates me and so everything is put in order. Even within the drawers, I have little containers to keep everything looking clean. Even the closets are tidy and clean. How did I let my business get so unorganized in the early days? I often analyze how and why this happened. My best understanding is that I was stretched so thin that I got overwhelmed and because the firm foundation was not assembled, my billing got unorganized. Have you ever seen when a chord or Christmas lights get all tangled and knotted up? That is how I felt my life, business, and billing was in those early days. Today, however, things are organized, simple, and in many ways on autopilot. Here is how I did it.

Step one is that I got signed up with a CRM. Remember, in the early days of my lawn business, money was tight. Now I simply use a CRM with all the bells and whistles and expanded features, back then I just rolled with a free one that only offered basic management services. One of those options that were available though was a credit card on file. For whatever reason, I was intimidated by this. How could I get all my customers to give me their credit card information? Thankfully, I had a track record of faithfulness and integrity with my customers, but I was still nervous to request such important information from my customers. What if there was identity theft and someone cleaned out their account and what if they would suspect it was me. Obviously, I would never think of doing such a thing, but I did not ever want to be in that situation where they could at least wonder if I were the source of any impropriety. These were real battles in my mind about transitioning my customers to card on file. What eventually pushed me over the edge and got me all in on this billing procedure was a flurry of my friends who had made this switch in their business and were loving it. The benefit of having my customer's card on file is that on the agreed-upon date, I could charge their card the agreed-upon amount, and just like that the money was on its way electronically to my account. 1-2 business days later and it showed up in my business checking account. This was so much easier than opening up the greasy grill looking for my check or driving through Atlanta traffic to check my PO Box to see if the check arrived. This was a lot easier than the game of phone tag and emails tracking down payments. Other business owners that I respected had successfully stored their customers' cards on file and I was determined to go for it.

Now, at the same time, I made this transition, I doubled down on another billing practice of receiving payment before we actually provided the service for lawn maintenance. I previously had this set up with some of my customers but many others would pay me after the fact. Honestly, I probably went a little overboard with the dramatic overhaul in changing all my customers to prepay and card on file. But, the truth is I should have had this system in place since day one, but I just did not know any better. And so I drew the line in the sand. Any new customer who desires us to provide their weekly lawn maintenance must store their card on file and we will charge their card the first of each month. This was clearly communicated in writing and to my surprise implemented without a hiccup. My fears of customers being hesitant to put their card on file were exaggerated. Customers appreciated how simple and easy that would be for them. They did not have to worry about taking the time to pay me each month, but one time they inserted their card information online, and then it was on autopilot from there. Easy peasy--set it and forget it! As consumers we are already used to this, Whether it is our cell phone bill, cable, vehicle insurance, it is a lot easier to just put it on auto-pay. That way we do not have to worry about late fees or interruption to our service because we forgot to pay the bill.

To clarify, so there is not any confusion, prepay with a card on file is how I set it up for lawn maintenance customers. But, what about those high-profit landscape installs? This is where I implemented a third, third, and third payment plan. For easy math, let's say we put in a bid for a $10,000 job. That is about average for a front yard makeover in the community where we perform services. What I will do is send the bid. It would read Project 1 - and then I would go in detail about what we were providing. How many square feet of sod, how many yards of mulch, the names, and amounts of plants, trees, and boulders we would be installing. And then they would see one price. We do not itemize the price, but the customer only sees the one rate for the total job. For our example here we will say it comes out to $10,000. In the bid, I explain we will store your card on file and we will charge it for one-third or $3,333 as a down payment to get on our schedule. I give them the most accurate forecast of when we should get started, but typically we are booked out for weeks. And so when they receive the bid if they accept the job they will respond and then fill out their card info and I will then charge it for the first installment of a third of the total job cost. Then, I explain that on the first day we actually get started working on the job, we will charge the next installment of a third or $3,333 in our example. This is the day we arrive with our shovels, Toro Dingo, and get to work. Then, I explain the payment of the final third will be due on the day of completion of the job before our crew leaves the property. In other words, before we drive away that day completing the job their card will be charged the final $3,334.

Nearing job completion I will communicate with the customer so hopefully they can be home the afternoon we finish for the final walk-through and make sure they are very happy with the quality of our work. It is always best to do that walk through and make sure the customer is a happy camper before charging that final third. The benefit of a 33 percent deposit, 33 percent on start, and the final upon completion is that we received two-thirds of the amount of the job before we even start. This helps with cash flow because we always stay ahead of the game. We are really only on the hook for 33% and since our goal is to have a profit margin slightly higher than that we will have received the amount upfront to cover the job materials, labor, and overhead to complete the job. And thankfully, to this day we have never had an issue with getting paid in full for a landscape installation. This is because there were clear payment instructions upfront, we successfully stored our customer's card on file, and of course doing excellent work by providing our customer the exact service we agreed to.

What was not as successful or smooth was eliminating those knots, untangling those chords of getting my old lawn maintenance customers on board with the new updated policy of prepay and card on file. In hindsight, perhaps I could have navigated this process more smoothly, but it was honestly a struggle. Why fix what isn't broken was some of my customers' thoughts? Some of them were used to me texting them the night before our arrival reminding them to tape the check to the front door, or put the check under the mat , or put the check in the grill. Most of my customers over the years had become good friends and I think a lot of them enjoyed the personal touch. The problem was it was not an efficient way to operate a business by all of my over communication and hoops I was constantly jumping through to get paid. Perhaps, my customer's would be missing out on some of that friendship element that I brought to the table, but if I could eliminate those texts and trips to the backyard to flip open the grill looking for the check with a more automated system then it would improve my business and honestly be more convenient for the customer.

The reality was for some customers I spent way too much time notifying them when we were coming so that they could make sure our check was there. Then, we would arrive, they would be at work, and when I would flip open the grill or lift up the mat to get our check sometimes it would not be there. Yes, there was the occasional time it was there and it got blown into the bush (that did happen), but oftentimes the check was missing, Then, I would have to send another text and I would receive their delayed reply with how sorry they were that they forgot and they would pay double next service. It was a broken system. I should have never fallen into these poor tendencies, but I did and I needed to fix it. So one by one, I contacted my customers and let them know I was switching to the card on file and pre-pay. I did lose some customers in this transition, some understood and got set up on my new plan, and unfortunately, I allowed a few to be grandfathered in and we continued with the check on the door system. Eventually, I was able to bring everyone up to speed and now things are all aligned with the new policy. Prepay card on file, no exceptions. You do not go to McDonald's, order your big mac, eat it, and then tell them you will pay next time you are in the restaurant. You place your order, pay, then receive your Big

Mac and fries. We don't question McDonald's procedure, you may question the ingredients in the food, but if you want your meal you pay upfront then receive your food. It is simple and straightforward. When we get confident in our billing policy, our customers will feel comfortable and we can get the system automated and operating efficiently so that we can give our attention to matters other than collecting payments.

15

NOW IS THE TIME FOR HIGHER PROFIT MARGINS

One definition of vanity is: without real significance, value, or importance, baseless or worthless. As a business owner, there is nothing more frustrating than investing our time and energy into doing work only for it to be unprofitable. There were some jobs I did that when I analyzed the numbers I actually lost money. Think about it, I invested time, energy, wear and tear on my equipment, and when it was all said and done I lost money. It would have been more profitable to sit on the couch and watch TV or play a video game. Not that I recommend being lazy, but the point is if we are not laser-focused on our pricing we can work in vain.

Mentally, I fell into a trap of using an employee's mindset in the early days of my business. In college, I worked in the dining hall. And so for a few hours each day, I would work and in return, they would calculate how many hours I worked at my pay rate then subtract any employee meals I consumed and the taxes for the pay period to generate my paycheck. I began to realize my pay was determined by how many hours I worked. This can be a dangerous mindset for a business owner.

As I started my lawn business, I would work long hours pushing that raggedy mower all day. I was working many more hours than I was used to at my jobs in high school and college. The problem is when you are a small business owner the equation is not as simple as it is as an hourly employee. My long hours working in the Georgia heat did not equate to the amount earned on my paycheck. It was up to me to calculate my overhead, job materials, taxes, and make sure I was charging the customer enough that by the time I paid all my expenses and taxes that I was still profitable. Ten years into owning a business I am a lot more intentional and aware of this, but in the early days, I was underpricing my services. With no bookkeeper in the beginning and really not much insight into data analysis, I was essentially working in vain. Once I did finally hire an accountant, she jokingly explained to me that I would have probably made more money that year if I would have worked at McDonald's. It was not funny, because that specific year, the math would have backed up that claim. I worked long hard hours, but because I was not charging enough, my business was on life support. Ultimately, what saved me in those days was I had other income coming in keeping me afloat. But, it was not until I increased my efficiency and raised my prices that I was able to transfer from a net loss to a net profit. And in those days the profit was slim, but now the goal is to continue boosting those profit margins and experience prosperity.

One of the great components of capitalism is competition.

Strong competition drives prices down. As a consumer, this is a blessing. For example, if we are searching for a new mower, there are so many great options. And because there are several companies competing for our purchase the prices are in our favor. If it was a monopoly and only one company sold mowers, the price could be outrageously high.

As business owners, we need to understand that competition drives prices lower. If we are not careful our prices could dip to low placing us in the red rather than in the black. Each industry is a little different, but in the niche of lawn care maintenance providers, there is very minimal room for error. The prices have been driven so low, one professional described it as "a race to the bottom." On a recent episode of the Green Industry Podcast I interviewed Troy Clogg who owns one of the top landscape and snow removal companies in Michigan. Troy explained something that was very alarming. He emphasized that the price for lawn maintenance has not increased much over his last forty years in the industry. A $25 lawn from the 1980s may only be a $30 lawn today. However, operational expenses have nearly quadrupled over the last several decades. A $13,000 truck back in the day is now selling for $52,000. Expenses for lawn and landscape professionals continue to rise, but not at the same rate people are willing to pay for lawn services. This creates a huge problem and is the reason why so many lawn businesses fail. In order to make it long term and stay in the black, efficiency and pricing has to be on point.

There were a few things that happened to help break up this log jam and help me swim into new waters of higher profitability. The first is a solid reputable bookkeeper. I heard others say you can not afford not to have a bookkeeper. I should have listened, but in my efforts to save money I did not. Truth is, I would have probably saved so much more money and earned more money if I would have hired a quality bookkeeper sooner. The bookkeeper I currently work with does not just organize my transactions, but they really help me analyze my reports and the pulse of my business. In many ways they are like a financial coach to me. My NFL coaching friends spend their Mondays in the film room analyzing their players' performance from the previous game day. Having a solid bookkeeper has helped me really dive into the numbers and truly analyze how my business is really doing. Some of these review calls can be sobering when the numbers are not as good as they should be. But, the numbers tell a story. And they share factual information on how the business is really doing. Before I had a bookkeeper I stayed distracted and unorganized and was able to avoid facing reality. Since I now work with a quality bookkeeping service, that has the heart to help me succeed, I am able to face the truth head-on. Sometimes this analysis can be a time to celebrate success and great profit margins. Other times it can be a swift kick in the butt and a wake-up call to make needed changes ensuring the bottom line is healthy.

In addition to a quality bookkeeping service, having other friends who are business owners keeping me accountable has been super helpful. I am not talking about those superficial acquaintances who you have plastic conversations with and who exaggerate how business is booming. I am talking about real friends who will dive into the data with me. In this Instagram highlight reel culture, it's easy to look like a winner. But, what do the checking and savings accounts actually look like? What do the profit and loss statements actually show? What is really going on? I am not suggesting sharing this information with too many people. Thankfully I have been blessed with some trustworthy friends, who are business owners, that I am able to chat with about real numbers. Iron sharpening iron. Friends who fight for me, who want to see me succeed for real.

You have probably heard the phrase "know your numbers." I would also add "know your market." A key contributor to seeing a hike in my profit margins is gaining knowledge of what prices other companies in the community I work in are charging. When I started I would not dare ask what my competition was charging. Everything seemed to be a big secret. The other companies that worked in the neighborhood seemed like they were not too friendly. One day I watched a Stanley "Dirt Monkey" Genadek YouTube video. He offered some insightful perspectives about actually being friends with the competition. To give a quick summary of the rather lengthy video, don't be afraid to have candid conversations with those who work in the same area. Honestly, that video alone provided me a paradigm shift. I started to open up and break the ice with some of the other companies working in the neighborhood. It began with waving and smiling while I worked and they worked across the street or drove by. Since I predominantly worked in one gated community I would see the same other companies working each day. And with a little bit of discernment, I could sense who was the foreman or business owner. In an organic way, I would start to talk. Introducing myself, drum up some small talk about the weather, equipment set up, but eventually, I would begin to talk about pricing. Once the relationship was established I was blunt and direct in my questions. How much do you charge for that property? Do you bill per service or per month? How much do you charge for a bale of pine straw? How much do you charge per yard of mulch? To my surprise, the majority of these other lawn and landscape professionals would answer. There seemed to be mutual respect and understanding that I was not going to undermine them and intrude with their customers or vice versa, but in a way, we had each other back. Keeping an eye out on each other's equipment and establishing these friendships where we began to openly discuss numbers and share customer stories (there were some interesting stories, to say the least, country clubs have some drama). Perhaps, because I was the new kid on the block, guys were just trying to help me out with the honest answers. But, those conversations helped me. Quickly realizing my rates were too low I was beginning to piece together enough information to begin to understand my market. You must know your specific market to understand profitable pricing.

As we compile our overhead, factor in the salary we want to personally earn, and consider market rates we can begin to hone in on the prices we should offer. Because people will be reading this book from all over the world in the years ahead, I do not want to give any outdated information about exact pricing and numbers. I do have our pricing playbook available at greenindustrypodcast.com that shares the exact pricing that we charge for lawn and landscaping services and will continue updating it in the future.

The last point I want to emphasize about profitable pricing is that efficiency is everything. The faster we can get the job done in a quality way the better. The trap is to overpay for equipment by telling ourselves we need it to increase efficiency. But, there is a way to really analyze the return on our investment. It is necessary to have a strategy and game plan to acquire the tools and equipment to maintain an efficient operation. Whether it is billing, communication, or the actual performance of services, dialing in on the most efficient way to get the job done is vital. Just raising our customer's price is not enough. We must also increase our productivity and get work done in a timely and economical manner.

Raising rates is an important component to maintaining profitable pricing. Just the other day I was reminiscing with my childhood friend Justin Rush who is also a small business owner. We were discussing our high school memories and how we remembered going to Wendy's after enjoying a day at the golf course. The go-to order back in the day was the Junior Bacon Cheeseburger for only $0.99. Justin was explaining to me over the phone that he was just at Wendy's with his wife and realized the Junior Bacon Cheeseburger is now $2.00. He told his wife, "I remember when those used to be $0.99!" Did Wendy's double the price? Technically, yes, but it was not overnight. It was a gradual, consistent, increase over the years and we never really noticed. Have you ever heard about the study they did with the frog in boiling water? When they put a frog in boiling water, the frog immediately leaps out. However, when they put the frog in room temperature water and slowly increase the temperature the frog never notices. Did we really take note of when Wendy's bumped the price of the Junior Bacon Cheeseburger? Maybe a few people noticed, but the masses probably did not give much attention to it because the rate increase was so small. But fast forward 15 years later and the price doubled.

I remember one of my first lawn maintenance customers. It was my friend's home. He lived in the $1.25 million dollar home on the golf course. I started out charging the rate of $45 per service. However, after five years of doing his property, I was still charging $45. What I should have done is after that first season, I should have informed the customer for the upcoming season there would be a slight rate increase and the new price was $48. I was doing a good job, they were satisfied, surely they would have accepted the slight rate increase. Then after that second season heading into the spring of season three, I should have bumped it again a few bucks. At this point, I could have been charging $51. If I would have consistently slightly raised the rate $3 each season, by year six I would have been charging $60 per service. I could have been staying ahead of inflation and increasing my profit. However, in those early years of my business, I did not understand this concept and I had a poverty mentality in many ways. I left a lot of money on the table because I was not consistently raising my rates. Please let me clarify, I am not saying a $3 rate increase per year is the proper number for the increase. That was just an example to drive home my point and emphasize that a small increase each year is reasonable and customers should be understanding and continue employing your services. When we price the property accurately from day one, then consistently raise prices, we can stay profitable. But, if we come in with too low of a price out of the gate we can really get ourselves in trouble. And if we fail to raise rates, then it will be hard to make the request to raise the rate from $45 per maintenance to $60 per maintenance. That may get rejected, but if we consistently gradually raise the rate, customers begin to get used to the slight rate adjustment. We probably still eat at Chick-fil-a or Wendy's even though they consistently raise the price of those spicy chicken sandwiches. The key takeaway is to price our properties accurately on day one and then be faithful to stay ahead of inflation with those steady rate increases. Across the board, I raise my rates annually. After 2-3 years, our customers will get trained up that this is all standard, and will come to expect their slight rate adjustment at the start of each season.

16

FOR PROFESSIONAL LOOKING TURF

I quickly learned that the customers I serviced in the gated community had high expectations. By high expectations I mean no weeds in the turf, along with many other specific requirements to keep their properties looking pristine. In the early stages of my career all I really knew about how to get rid of the weeds was to put a glove on my hand and pull them out ...lol! Well, that's what my mother taught me to do as a kid. My chore was to do the "weeding". This is where I would walk around the garden beds and pull out, by hand all the weeds.

I have multiple friends that solely offer weed control and fertilizer services and they make bank! They actually used to offer lawn maintenance and landscape enhancement services, but found it to be more profitable to only do weed control. Some of them offer 7 applications a year while others offer 8, but the bottom line is their bottom line is healthy.

Now, the reason I started to offer weed control services was because my customers were inquiring about it and I did not want to lose their business. The problem though, was that I did not have a clue what I was doing. This resulted in many costly mistakes.

My first confrontation with these irritating weeds was in March my second year. I was still a rookie, and uneducated in understanding when weeds germinate and grow etc. And so that March, my customer who had the 1.25 million golf course home had their turf completely weed infested. I was so overwhelmed. I knew I needed to get this taken care of immediately or they may let me go. This is when I called my mentor Kenny. He bailed me out, and came over and took care of removing the weeds and getting down some pre emergent to prevent future weeds. Being the profitable business man he is though, he explained he could not oversee my properties' weed control services. He did however connect me to the manager where he purchases all his products. And so being the rookie I was, I would constantly go to his supplier with the pictures of the weeds and get the correct product to spot spray them and try to keep my customer happy. I did have some attrition because I was not too skilled at keeping these properties weed free.

When I would lose a customer because our work was not up to par it would bother me. I did not like that feeling, and it energized me to learn and become more professional. I took classes at the County Extension office to learn more about weed control and get the proper licensing, etc. As the years rolled on, I truly was learning the ropes and understanding that the proper applications, at the right times, helped the lawns stay relatively weed free. That was good news, but the bad news was this aspect of my company was not profitable for several reasons. One, my original prices were too low, and so the profit margins were not there when you add in all my product costs for the correct products to apply. One day when I went to the warehouse to show the manager some new pictures of weeds I was battling, he gave me some bold advice. He explained to me that he thought it might be time to sub contract this work out to a professional who is trustworthy and who could maintain my customers properties with excellence. This would reduce my headaches of constantly worrying about the various weeds and timing of the applications etc. I listened and made the move, hiring my friend Russell Skippers company to take care of all our properties. I continued having my customers pay me directly and then Russell would bill me separately. It worked out, the yards are weed free, the customers are happy, and once I finally raised my prices to the proper, profitable rate, it was a win for everyone.

17

IT PAYS TO KNOW GREAT SUBCONTRACTORS

Some of my first experiences with subcontractors were very sour. I quickly realized if a customer wants you to mow their grass, they are likely going to request you take care of other aspects of their lawn, landscape, and even their home. I was being asked if we did fertilizer and weed control? Do you plant trees? Do you install seasonal flowers? Can you fix our irrigation? Do you do lighting? Do you clean gutters? The list just keeps on going. People assume if you are the lawn boy or lawnmower man then you are probably a handyman that can repair anything inside or outside the house.

When starting my business I still had a poverty mentality and I was in a desperate spot in life. And so it was my tendency to answer yes whenever a customer asked me if I could... fill in the blank. After a while of being the yes man, the math was not working, as I would take on offering additional services. I was losing money. In addition to that, I was also running out of time. It would be getting dark and I still had so much work to do. I would just repeat the process. Realizing I could not do it all alone, I was eventually going to need to get some subcontractors to help out until I either got the right equipment and knowledge to provide more services or until I had the gumption to say no to certain services.

One of these first sour subcontractor stories was with an irrigation guy. To protect his real name, we will just call him Rick. The situation was I was doing one of my first sod jobs. It was about a $3,500 job and I was making many mistakes on this job. First, the price was way too low. There was also miscommunication. I originally thought we were just expected to sod the front yard area in front of the house, but then the homeowner mentioned the side yard. I did not measure that area and was embarrassed and so I just threw that in as complementary to the price already given the customer. Long story short, we lost money on the job when you factor in job materials, labor, and basic overhead. It pains me to this day to remember doing jobs at a loss, but it happened. The mistake on the job was not only in the pricing.

Since it was one of my first sod jobs, I did not do a thorough job checking that the irrigation system was properly functioning so that once we installed the sod, they would be able to properly water the sod. It was in the middle of summer, and those hot 90 degree days can dry out fresh sod fast. I did at least ask the homeowner if they had irrigation and if it worked, they said, yes, but unfortunately, I took their word for it and did not double-check to investigate myself that each head was working properly. You probably see where this is going.

As we are completing the project in what seems to be record-breaking Georgia heat the homeowner notifies me the irrigation system was not working. I got flustered. The homeowner works out of town and so he could not hand water it. And it was five pallets, which would be a lot to hand water even if they were in town. It seemed like the only logical thing was to fix the irrigation system. At the time I could switch out a sprinkler head, but the repair was a lot more than that. At least one rotor was out and the repair was beyond my pay grade at the time. On top of all that I was beyond stressed out because as we were doing the sod job, we were falling behind on so much other work and I also had a part-time job at the time. Things were falling apart. I got on the phone and started going through my directory calling around to see if I could find someone who knew someone who could come fix this irrigation so the sod we just planted would not die. I could not find anyone.

Finally, I called an irrigation store that sells the irrigation products like the heads and pipes and such and asked if they did repair work. They did not, they just sold the products, but they said they could connect me with a subcontractor that buys a bunch of products from them. Being desperate I said please give me the guy's number and so they did and I called Rick. Perhaps, I could have had a better poker face with my initial call with Rick. But, I was tired, I was losing money, I was stressed out, my life was a mess and Rick could probably hear it in my voice. I told him the situation of how we were laying down five pallets of zoysia sod in this 92-degree heat and that the irrigation system was not working. Rick explained how his schedule was full and could not help me. I asked ole Rick if he knew anyone else that I could call because if this sod died I was going to have to replace it. Side note, that was another mistake I made, I do not warranty sod any more, but when I was a rookie I did. Anyway, Rick replied that if I paid him extra he could expedite his schedule and come out and see what he could do.

And so Rick came out and fixed the irrigation and then I was at the fork in the road. Do I pay Rick or does the homeowner pay him? I did not break the irrigation. When I asked if they had working irrigation the homeowner said yes. Should the homeowner pay for it or me? One lesson I learned from that mistake was I would always personally check myself in the future before doing sod if the irrigation was properly working. The homeowner and I had an awkward conversation about who will pay Rick for the irrigation repair and they agreed they would pay for it. This is where things got frustrating. Not only was Rick very arrogant and rude, but his prices were outrageous. The homeowners were furious when they got the bill. They were mad at Rick because it was highway robbery. And they were mad at me because I set up Rick to come out and do the repair. They thought they could have found someone more reasonable.

That was obviously the last time I communicated with Rick. He was very unprofessional. This was a wake-up call to me though, that I needed to start finding some allies and more reputable subcontractors. What if I needed an irrigation repair in the future that was beyond my skill set. Who would I call?

Those first few years my subcontractor list was a revolving door like Cleveland Browns quarterbacks before Baker Mayfield. It seemed like there were a lot of Rick's out there. But, that is when the tide started to turn. I remember receiving a Facebook message from a lady who listened to my radio program. She mentioned that her husband owned an irrigation company and that if I ever needed work done to call him and she shared his number. Well, ironically, I had just bid on a $17,000 job with a lot of irrigation involved. If this guy were any good, it would be perfect timing. I called him, his name is Rich, and he showed up, gave me a reasonable quote, and completed the work in a professional manner. Hallelujah! I finally found a reliable irrigation subcontractor! I later found out he also did lighting work. And so you better believe I saved Rich's number. And the good fortunes seemed to continue from there I eventually met Scotty who does a great job grinding stumps. My friend Chance would begin to be my go-to guy for tree work that was outside my insurance coverage. I went on to get teamed up with Joe who would do large grading jobs, and slowly but surely I started connecting and networking with solid subcontractors. Folks who had integrity, common sense, professionalism, and made me look good. What I mean by that is when they were on my customer's properties they got the job done with excellence, and my customers appreciated that, and it would come back to positively affect me. Quite the opposite of my experience with Rick where the outcome was that my customer was mad at me.

I say all that to say it is crucial to have a great line up of subcontractors who are honest and dependable. This assembly did not happen overnight, and it did not happen in a calendar year. It happened over time as I weeded out the bad ones. But once you find a good one in their respective field, understand that is rare and go above and beyond to keep them around. Whether it's getting them Christmas gifts, or just sincere compliments I realized it was important to stay in good standing with great subcontractors. And of course, make sure you pay them on time, every time. If you are reliable, they will likely be as well.

The ultimate compliment about my subcontractors came from the Atlanta Falcons Defensive Coordinator! The Defensive Coordinator at the time was one of my customers and he invited me to sit on the back porch with him and his wife one evening to chat business. We had recently remodeled his entire front yard. We gutted everything and planted all new plants, trees, sod, flowers, mulch, etc. They were happy customers. As we enjoyed the sunset in this beautiful backyard he complimented how I had this All-Star lineup of subcontractors. They had experienced the quality of work and character from Joe who did their grading, Chance who chopped down several trees and limbed up many others, they met Jamie who designed and installed all their new trees, boulders, plants, flowers, etc. and they even met Scotty who grinds the stumps. It meant a lot to me when Coach Smith acknowledged the spirit of excellence behind the subcontractors and he also shared with me several ways I could continue to build my company into something special because I had such a reliable set of people I worked with to produce quality work.

18

STRAIGHT TALK ABOUT
RELATIONAL INTELLIGENCE

The story of how I discovered one of my customers was the Defensive Coordinator for the Atlanta Falcons is actually quite comical! As I have mentioned throughout this book, in those early years of establishing my lawn and landscape business my schedule was very full. Although I enjoy both playing and watching sports, especially football, the reality was I just was not paying too much attention to sports in those days. My favorite team the Cleveland Browns were disappointing and so I just stayed in my lane and worked on building my business.

In those days we actually started our Saturday lawn maintenance at 8:00 am. I was mindful that it was not the best etiquette to do someone's maintenance that early on a Saturday morning and so we would always start with this house where the homeowner actually lived in California. They had their vacation home in this fine Atlanta neighborhood and so we would always do that property first thing Saturday morning. On this particular Saturday morning, while my worker Robert got started on the maintenance, I ran over to the Home Depot to pick up some supplies and that is when my phone started ringing. It was Robert and so I answered and could immediately sense something was wrong. Robert was calling to inform me that the next door neighbor lady was furious that we kept waking them up every Saturday morning.

I realized this was a great inconvenience for her and so when I returned from the Home Depot I walked over to her house to apologize. She explained that they have guests in town every weekend for the football games and we consistently disturb the peace with our loud lawn equipment every Saturday morning. I offered my apologies and told her we would reroute our schedule so that it would not happen again. Then something shifted. The lady who was once frustrated about the noise disturbance was now seeming very delightful. She then stunned me and asked if I could give her a quote for her property. She showed me the areas where her current provider was not doing a good job and complimented the quality work we did for her neighbor. In a wild turn of events, I ended up giving a quote and she hired us!

A few weeks later after we had been maintaining their property, I remembered she had mentioned that they had guests over every weekend for the football games. So one day when her husband was out in the front yard, attempting some small talk, I asked him what football team he cheered for? I just assumed their guest would come in town for the Georgia Bulldog games, as SEC football is a big deal here in Atlanta. When I asked the question he just smirked and looked at me. He replied, "The Atlanta Falcons!" After pausing, he then said, "I am the Defensive

Coordinator!" Oh my gosh. I was both embarrassed and excited at the same time. I was embarrassed that I did not know this about him and I was excited that one of my customers was the Defensive Coordinator for the Atlanta Falcons. Over the next several years our relationship blossomed and this family blessed me in many ways. They took me to several Falcons games and referred me to several other NFL players and coaches who lived in their community. Atlanta is a hot spot for the rich and famous because you can get a lot more house for a very reasonable price. Many athletes have homes here even though they live in other cities during the season. Over the years I've had the privilege of servicing players and coaches from the Atlanta Falcons, Arizona Cardinals, Los Angeles Chargers, Buffalo Bills, and New York Giants. This was a great responsibility and opportunity, but it was also a huge learning curve.

When you are rich and famous, unfortunately, you can attract a lot of people who want something from you. It may be a hand-out for money, or tickets, or a networking connection. It took me a while to truly understand how all this works, but one day I made a gigantic mistake that helped me learn this lesson in a hurry.

It was Christmas season and I was inside one of my customer's homes as they were writing my check. This was obviously before I updated to better practices in my billing. I noticed what looked like a store laid out all across the sunroom. There were auto-graphed jerseys everywhere. Julio Jones and Matt Ryan signed jerseys, signed helmets, all kinds of apparel like hoodies, hats, and t-shirts. And this is where I put my foot in my mouth and the Lord sharply disciplined me. What happened is that as I saw all these incredible Falcons autographed gear I thought of my cousin in Ohio who was a huge Atlanta Falcons fan. I had the idea of how much he would love an autographed Julio Jones or Matt Ryan jersey. And here I noticed countless pieces of signed merch all over the place. And so I blurted out, "Do you think you could get me a jersey?" And this is when I truly had one of my most distinct encounters with God. He instantly disciplined me. It felt like before I even got the words off my tongue, the Lord internally shouted to me, "Never ask a question like that again!" My customer slightly uncomfortably answered, sure, if you ever want anything I can meet you at the team store where we get 30%. She explained that even the players and coaches have to buy their own products, but they do get a 30% family discount.

And so my customer handed me the check for our landscaping services for that month and I was on my way out the door. When I got to my truck I felt like I got a spanking from the Lord. He continued in His love to rebuke me and explain why he said never to ask for something like that again. You see rich and famous people often do not like it when people ask them for stuff. It happens so frequently that it gets annoying to them and they can feel like people are just using them. I learned that if I was going to get exalted and promoted within these circles of influential people, I needed to carry myself with great professionalism. I needed to let my excellent work, professional communication, and integrity be what opened the doors and opportunities. But, at no time, for any circumstance, was I to ask for anything. It was a very clear instruction to my soul from God, do not ask for autographs, or pictures, or tickets, or anything of that nature. But, I was to be a friend, and seek ways where I can be a blessing to these prominent people and most of all stay in my lane.

This has been super helpful over the years. Other than that mistake, one December day, I was able to provide value to these influential and wealthy people. Over time that builds great trust with them. They trusted that I could provide the services I was committed to providing and that they could trust me to be around their homes and guests and that I would be professional, exercising basic relational intelligence. The interesting reality is, I ended up getting tons of swag and apparel, tickets, and all kinds of opportunities, but I never initiated any of it. It came from my customers when I was not expecting it. I just kept my head down, "cutting that grass and making that cash," staying in my lane. My customers made it all happen for me. They kept referring me to their friends and often gave me opportunities to go to the Falcons games and various other sporting and social events.

Trust is very important. If we want people of elite status to trust us, we need to be on top of our game. Dress and talk in a professional manner, do excellent work, and be mindful of how you can be a blessing to this customer. Most people are so selfish and focus on themselves, but that will backfire. The secret when serving the rich and famous is to think about how I can be a blessing to them. I've also discovered this principle works with clients up and down the social-economic ladder.

It is not necessary for building a profitable business that you need to have rich and famous clients. And not all famous people are rich, and not all rich people are famous. Actually, you would not even know most millionaires are millionaires. They are not flashy. As a notorious bank robber once told Larry King in response to the question, "Why did you rob the bank?", he replied, "Because that is where the money is!" I just found that it is better to service neighborhoods where the money is. Perhaps you live in an area where there are not luxurious neighborhoods like the one I service in Atlanta. As long as we provide a quality service at a profitable price, we can still make our business successful whether it's in rural Southern Ohio like Caleb Auman or perhaps, like me, you are in a metro area of a major city. My point is if we do come across the rich and famous, do not be selfish, but it's best to serve them well and stay in our lane.

19

CHOOSING THE RIGHT
COMPANY NAME

"A good name is more desirable than great riches; to be esteemed is better than silver or gold." - Proverbs 22:1. A good reputation is vital in building route density and a successful business. A good name is also important for a couple of reasons.

On episode #156 of the Green Industry Podcast, guest Nick Carlson shared how important the company's name is if you were to one day consider selling your company. I jokingly mentioned that I wish he would have shared that information with me a decade prior. I made some careless decisions in naming my business. However, Nick in his experience of selling a company, emphasized you want a name that the new buyer can effortlessly use to keep the company operating.

If I were to sell "Paul Jamison Lawn Care" the new business owner may have some issues with the current customers. Where is Paul? The name of the business was centered around me.

However, if the name of the business is more generalized, such as "Duluth Lawn Care" then the new owner can just keep business flowing. It is best practice not to have the name around a personality, but more so about the services offered. If I were to rename my business, I would probably select something like Sugarloaf Landscaping. Sugarloaf is the area where we work, and landscaping defines what we do, and this can have more value at the point of sale should I decide to sell the business one day.

Some would argue, just name it your last name. That does have some benefits, but the main drawback is at the point of sale. When I started my business, I was not beginning with the end in mind. I was not thinking or planning that I was going to build a big lawn and landscaping company and then sell it for top dollar. At that time, my mindset was more focused on how I was going to put gas in the 1997 accord and pay next month's rent. When I created my first set of business cards, I named my company "Paul Jamison Lawn Care." Shortly after that I went to the county offices and got my first business license and made things official as "Paul Jamison Lawn Care." In hindsight, I would have not selected that name, nor the second and third name of my company. Lol, that is right. I have changed the name three times. This was not good for branding, but it is another one of those rookie mistakes.

During my second year in business a friend of mine at church who was an entrepreneur asked me about my presence on Google. He was a sharp fellow. He had built and sold multiple businesses, and was very wealthy. He was excited for me on my entrepreneur journey. He kept drilling into my thoughts the importance of search engine optimization. And being the generous man he was, he said he was going to connect me with one of his employees who would build me a website for free. He had this grin on his face when sharing this with me because he knew "his guy" would help me see big results. And so that is exactly what he did. He connected me with his IT guy who built me a website. The predicament though was that the website guru said I needed to change my name. He wanted me to include the word lawn in my business name, he explained it would help boost me in the Google search engine optimization strategy. And so he chose, PJLAWN as my new company name, and made a great website pjlawn.com. This guy sure knew what he was doing because in a short amount of time I was ranking as a top three company in my local area. The phone was ringing off the hook, and the opportunities seemed endless. But, eventually it came to a screeching halt. My friend ended up transitioning companies and no longer employed the website guru, and my website eventually expired and then I created my third company under a different name.

Long story short, or as my friend Naylor says, short story long, I had three separate company names in less than ten years. Not wise, but I hope my mistake can be avoided by the new guys just launching their business. And one more observation to share, is don't try to get too cute with describing your business. When a company is "Reliable" Heating and Air, I usually get skeptical that they probably are not reliable. For you single guys out there, have you ever met a girl, and she tells you, I'm not crazy, lol, that's a red flag to run for the hills. Quality Roofing Company is probably not quality work lol.

I don't want to beat the dead horse, but I do think a well thought through name can earn you big money if you decide to sell your company one day. There are other components that will maximize how much you can sell the business for like detailed data, and the assistance of a reputable business broker, but I learned the hard way it's wise to have a business name that will boost your company's value if you decide to sell the company one day.

20

NOW THE REAL TRUTH ABOUT MARKETING

After being in this industry for a decade, I have learned word of mouth referrals from good customers is arguably the best form of marketing. Good people seem to be friends with other good people. And when you can organically start getting referred to within a solid network like that it has huge benefits. Position yourself to receive the wave of word of mouth referrals by making sure you are reliable and doing outstanding work. I have noticed wealthy clientele are not necessarily too worried about the price, they are more concerned about quality of work, professionalism, and reliability. Needless to say, the better job we do in every step of the process from the initial consultation, to the quote, to the actual work, and the billing, the more likely we are to be the beneficiary of great referrals. Strive for excellence in all that you do.

When a client I enjoy serving who is a pleasant customer refers to me one of their friends, I try my best to hop on that opportunity like Johnny on the Spot. That warm lead is typically well worth it. Then, when you do a good job for the new customer, word gets back to the original customer who did the referral and then they are happy that their friend is happy. It is a win-win-win situation. But, again, we need to stay hyper-focused on making sure we knock it out of the park with quality service, reliability, and professionalism.

The other great aspect of word of mouth referrals is that it is free marketing. We frequently discuss the subject of best marketing practices on the Green Industry Podcast. I hesitate to even mention some of these in a book, because with facebook ads, instagram ads, google ads, etc, the "best marketing buy" is constantly fluctuating as the prices and consumer attention is ever changing with the various social media platforms. I view our marketing strategy as a big pie. Growing up in Ohio, we would call a pizza a "pie," so maybe I should rephrase that as I view our marketing strategies as a big pizza. I like to have multiple slices as a part of the marketing plan. Email marketing, truck and trailer lettering, company uniforms, and online ads can all be slices. But, from my experience the granddaddy of them all has always been word of mouth referrals.

In football, a popular strategy is to strike while the iron is hot. An example of this is after a team gets an interception oftentimes they will then take a shot at the end zone. If successful, this can be a huge momentum shifter and game changer. This is my mindset with word of mouth referrals. Whenever, one of your favorite customers notifies you they shared your info with their friend, get ready! That very well could be gold! Be alert and ready to hop on that opportunity. Those warm/hot leads often convert to new customers because of trust. The prospective customer trusts you right out of the gate because of the quality recommendation they received from their trusted friend about you. Vetting customers can be challenging, but more times than not, the word of mouth referrals are worth our time and attention.

21

A DREAM REALIZED

In August 2018 I experienced some incredible blessings that forever changed my life. It all started with a generous gift from fellow lawn bro Bryan Ring from Stillwater, Minnesota. Bryan is a part of a mastermind group I am in with several other business owners. In this group, we chat about our businesses and life and encourage one another. That summer I had expressed some of my business struggles with the group about my lawn business. The consensus of the group is that I needed to double down on efficiency by upgrading equipment. It sounded like a good plan but I did not have the cash available to buy a new 48-inch mower and I was an avid Dave Ramsey listener and did not want to borrow money to make some equipment upgrades. At the time I had several mowers but the largest deck size was only 30 inches. As I was starting to commit to maintaining some larger properties this was not the most efficient way to get things done. Bryan was adamant that I should invest in a larger size mower. I was torn. Do I borrow the money to purchase a new 48 or 60-inch mower and then get a new sturdier trailer to go with it? Or do I drop my newer clients who have more square footage of turf than I am used to?

This is when I was blessed with a very generous message from Bryan Ring. He contacted me to tell me he would like to give me a 48-inch lawn mower and a trailer to go with it. This was a very generous gift. The only predicament is that Bryan lived all the way up in Minnesota and I am located down in Georgia. Bryan said the mower and trailer were all mine if I could just pick it up and drive it back to Georgia, all in all, it's about a 17-hour drive.

So I booked a flight from Atlanta to Minneapolis and was on my way to receive this generous gift from Bryan. This was a fun trip to Minnesota. He picked me up at the airport in the morning and we drove around Stillwater and he introduced me to his three crews and showed me several of the properties they take care of. We then went to Bryan's headquarters and he presented his generous gift to me of the 48-inch commercial lawn mower with a new engine and a 5x10 trailer with a new lighting system. We then stopped by the local U-Haul store where I picked up a U-Haul to transport the mower and trailer back to Georgia.

The next morning I woke up early, enjoyed a cup of coffee with Bryan, and then departed on the long journey back to Georgia. It was my first time visiting this area of the country and the weather was perfect on this August morning, so I was enjoying my commute home through Minnesota and Wisconsin. That is when I got to driving through Illinois and had a life-altering encounter. After passing through metro Chicago, I found myself driving through the Illinois countryside. I was surrounded by cornfields and the weather was picture perfect and that is when the life-changing vision began.

During the middle of the day the traffic was light. I briefly glanced at the radio and that is when this unique spiritual experience occurred. The best way I can explain it is that I had a vision. I was wide awake, somehow I did not crash but managed to continue to drive safely down the road, but my mind began to see what seemed like a movie. It was as if I got sucked into the radio and then saw the "movie" start playing. What I saw were men all over the place and they were listening to me talk. Men driving in their trucks, guys in their skid steers, in their shops, there were different scenes but the common denominator was that they were listening to me through their earbuds or truck's audio system. All of a sudden I snapped back and continued my commute down the Illinois highway when I heard that still small voice, "If you build it they will listen."

The encounter was startling. I quickly connected the dots. If I built a podcast, talking about business, people would listen. The vision and instructions were very simple, but then I began to overthink things. How would I have time to make a podcast? I was already overwhelmed with the day to day operations in my lawn and landscape business. On top of that, I was working on the weekends at the radio station. My schedule was full. I was trying to cut things out of my schedule and scale back. At this point in my life, I was still single and was thinking I needed to carve some space out of my schedule if I was going to pursue my future wife. The last thing that I needed to do was to add to my already full schedule a new project like starting a podcast. Before I had that vision, I had frequent thoughts about starting a podcast but would come to the same conclusion, I did not have the time to take on such an ambitious pursuit.

What I did have though, was a lot more hours until I arrived at the Indiana/Kentucky border where I was going to stay the night at my friend Rusty's home. And so I took it to the Lord in prayer. That is when I sensed the Lord challenge me to set the goal of 100 episodes. At that moment I had a negative tendency in my life where I would start a project and usually not finish it. I felt so stretched thin in those days and so it was hard to really gain traction on a mission or project. So I settled it in my heart and with the Lord in prayer that I would go for it. I would attempt to record 100 podcast episodes and then re-evaluate. The logic was if I only did 10 or 20 episodes I might get discouraged and stop. But, if I just go for it, create 100 episodes, then I would have a better gauge of if it was worth my time or if it was a flop.

The storyline instantly got even more interesting. After a long day driving through Minnesota, Wisconsin, Illinois, and Indiana I finally got to Rusty's home. It was beautiful weather on this summer night. Rusty at the time was not just a lawn care professional, but he also hosted a podcast. As we enjoyed some fellowship that evening I began to pick Rusty's brain about his podcasting career. The information Rusty shared was encouraging, helpful, and gave me some inspiration that I can do this.

The next morning, I hit the highway and was headed back to Georgia. I originally departed from Atlanta with the mission of picking up the 48-inch lawn mower and trailer, but as I was driving back home, it was with a new mission, launch this podcast! Shortly after getting back to Georgia, I experienced two blessings that helped successfully get the podcast off the ground. First, my friend, who many of you know as Mr. Producer was able to connect me with a recording studio where I would have temporary access to a professional mic and audio setup until I was able to build my own studio. This gave me the opportunity to get started on my podcasting immediately. Second, my friend Naylor came to Atlanta to interview me for his "Get To Know The Pro" series on YouTube. After he conducted his interview, I then interviewed him for my podcast. It was my first interview and he also encouraged me and filled me with confidence to give it my all in this effort of creating a podcast for the Green Industry. Naylor even helped guide me through the naming process and thus helped me land the name Green Industry Podcast. So in a very short amount of time after getting back from Minnesota the podcast was a reality. The Green Industry Podcast was available on Apple Podcast, Spotify, Google Podcast, Stitcher, and pretty much all major podcast platforms. And just like the Lord told me, if you build it they will listen. The listeners started pouring in. A big shout out and thank you to Brian Fullerton, who would frequently share the show with his large audience, and then others started sharing it, and eventually the podcast algorithms started to favor and recommend the show.

I was locked into the goal of 100 episodes. And so I kept creating. Episode after episode, the momentum was building and then I received one of the greatest blessings a podcaster could dream of receiving. If you listen to my show then you know Mr. Producer and his incredible skill set and comedy. On-air, he goes by Marty, but most people call him by his nickname Mr. Producer. He has almost 40 years in the broadcasting industry (He started in 1982) and has been a huge help with creating the show. With his assistance, I kept making episodes and eventually got to episode 100. I told myself once I arrived at episode 100 I would evaluate if I should continue and perhaps even reach out to sponsors. Surprisingly, sponsors began to reach out to me before episode 100, and by the time I published the 100th episode I already knew that the show was to continue. If you build it, they will listen. They were listening from Australia, New Zealand, all across Europe, Canada, and across the United States. Producing the show has been an incredible blessing, We have fun and learn so much valuable knowledge from our guests. Iron sharpens iron and we hope that those who listen are blessed.

22

MY GRANDPA'S TOOLS FOR BUSINESS SUCCESS

My grandpa Jim was one of my best friends. He recently passed away and so this chapter is not necessarily the easiest to share. But, what I learned from my grandpa was very valuable and I want to give it my best effort to impart what He shared with me.

Grandpa Jim had that entrepreneurial spirit along with an interesting compilation of life experiences. He grew up in the 1930s and experienced firsthand the economic effects of the Great Depression. I remember as a kid foolishly making fun of my grandpa because he would recycle his computer paper. I remember asking to use his computer for some school projects and when I would go to print out my documents and noticing on the backside of the paper was something that was previously printed. What my grandpa would do is after he printed something and did not need it anymore he would flip it over and fill it into the paper tray to use again. Meaning he would print the future document on the blank side. This was such a mystery to me. But, as I got older his explanation would make more sense as he explained that he did not want to waste the paper. You see his memories of the Great Depression had permanently taught him frugality and to appreciate the incredible wealth and opportunity we have in America. It was not that he did not have the money for new computer printer paper, it was that he did not want to waste anything. This frugality was evident in many ways.

I loved going out to eat with my grandparents. My grandpa loved mom and pop breakfast diners. I knew grandpa Jim loved coffee, but he would rarely order a coffee when we would go out to eat because he could not justify paying $2.00 for a cup of coffee. (I can only imagine what he would have thought about Starbucks prices). He ran the math and knew he could brew a hot cup of coffee at home for just a few cents. He was a businessman who understood margins and was old enough to actually know what it was like to experience extreme poverty and a financial depression.

My grandpa Jim spent the last few months of his life in a nursing home in North Canton, Ohio. Realizing that his days were likely nearing an end I was continually rearranging my schedule in an effort to travel to Ohio to spend some quality time with him. These were precious memories of sitting in his nursing home room and just chatting. Although his body was beginning to break down as he was 93, his memory was remarkably sharp. He would tell me detailed stories from the 1930s. One afternoon he went on a marathon and told the stories of his whole working career. He started with his first job at the cinema in downtown Canton where he made 25 cents per hour and he eventually shared with me the other jobs he worked and then ultimately about the filling station business he owned. It was so fascinating hearing about his incredible work ethic, those long cold winters working in the elements to keep his filling station up and running. I was intrigued by his wise financial decisions. See my grandpa was a wealthy man. Yes, he was frugal, but he was also extremely generous. It was his consistency of working hard, saving, and living on less than he made that lead to his wealth. He was a good man that left an inheritance to his children's children.

These conversations in the nursing home were not only inspiring but they were also convicting. My grandpa retired in the early 1990s, so the timeline of his working life was the 1930s through the 1980s. What convicted me was the principles he lived by and how faithful he was with the opportunities he had. See being an entrepreneur in this decade we have so many more opportunities. With the internet and advancements in travel and technology, the possibilities seem endless. The struggle is that since this reality is normal we can take it for granted and not realize how rare and special this time is. We can also get lazy and careless. Those $2 coffees that my grandpa despises, I had the habit of purchasing. The computer paper that my grandpa would recycle, I would waste.

My grandpa's work ethic, generosity, and frugality convicted me. But, it also encouraged me. It stretched and challenged me. He would work so hard and eventually save up and buy his home, which he moved into during the 1990s paying all cash. Years of working hard in the business he owned, living on way less than he made and always saving money allowed him to get the house with no mortgage payment. He was also able to invest money in the stock market to watch it grow and grow in his retirement years. He showed me the old fashioned way. He showed me the blueprint. He got me to ask myself the tough questions, how can I be more profitable? How can I be more frugal? How can I be a better saver? How can I be a better investor? How can I be more generous? How can I make sure I continue the legacy and leave an inheritance to my children's children?

23

NO LIMITS

Perhaps the greatest transformation from my first decade in business is the change in mindset I have had from poverty to abundance. When I started my lawn and landscape business I had a poverty mentality. This was partially why I was underpricing jobs and it was having a negative effect on the way I conducted business. Today my mentality is radically different. I believe the Lord wants my cup overflowing, that I would have more than enough, an abundance.

A turning point is when I heard Rabbi Daniel Lapin explain about candles. When one candle is lit, if it then connects with another candle, the second candle will start burning while the original candle continues to burn. It is a win-win situation and this is how business should be. When I had the poverty mind-set I thought that if a customer paid me, then their candle would go out as mine started to burn. But that is a lie! When I provide a quality service at a reasonable rate then my customer pays me certificates of appreciation or in other words money. But it is a win-win! My customer had a need. They needed their lawn mowed, or landscape improved. Now they may not have the time, expertise, or tools to perform the service. So they call on me. I show up and do a great job, Now my customer is blessed. Their grass is cut, their property is looking fresh and they are happy. Then, they paid me and I am blessed. It is a win-win.

When a business owner has a poverty mentality, they can think that during the transfer one's candle goes out. But it does not have to. Business can and should be a win-win! Profit is a blessing. Can some pervert it and get greedy? Yes, but I trust by staying on our knees in prayer and staying surrounded by quality well-charactered people, we can keep our hearts free from greed and the love of money.

Money in itself is not evil. Money is actually a powerful tool and resource. It can pay for our shelter and transportation, purchase our food and clothing, and even be enjoyed. In a football game the team that scores the most points wins. How do we measure winning in business? There are many definitions that vary depending on who you ask. I think a quality reputation is in part a way you win in business. When people view us as integral and excellent at the services we provide that is certainly a blessing, I also think winning is being profitable. As long as we are operating our business with integrity, honesty, and excellence then I think part of how we measure success is the bottom line. The higher the profits the better. We are blessed to be a blessing.

When I began to view profit as a worthy goal it helped improve how diligent and careful I became in my business decisions. It helps me to pause and really consider how this will affect the bottom line? Is this a wise decision? I still have the scars and wounds of working for a net loss and in vain. It is important to make the most of each moment and opportunity and be as profitable as possible.

Integrity, honesty, and profit is not the only way I measure success. How we treat people is important as well. Jesus taught us to treat others the way we want to be treated. That is so simple yet so profound, the essence of reverse engineering. How do you want to be treated? Very well. We like when people are respectful, kind, and caring. It is important that we keep that in mind in our pursuit of profit. Along the journey, let's treat all those we encounter the way we want to be treated.

24

PUTTING GOD FIRST

Out of all the lessons learned through my first decade in business, the next one I am about to share is by far the most important lesson. And let me be clear, I am still in progress with this one. I have not "arrived" at the destination so to speak, but am still on the journey. But, the bottom line is, the Lord humbled me, and reminded me that I desperately need Him. God is very interested in the details of our lives and He even used some of the low points and failures in my business to get my attention. He did this to remind me that I am not as smart as Him and that keeping Him first and leaning on His grace, wisdom, and guidance is of utmost importance in my life.

In 2004 my life dramatically was transformed by the LORD. And for the next couple of years after that, I was laser-focused on getting to know God and being very intentional about honoring Him in my decisions. Fast forward a decade or so later, and that fire had begun to grow dim. Now I still loved the Lord. I knew the songs, I knew the language, and I was even doing ministry on

Sundays. But, if you could really see into the depth of my soul you would have found that I was distracted. I was not necessarily distracted by sin. But, I was distracted with busyness, I was fragmented with my maxed out schedule and began to slowly make some decisions that the Lord would eventually discipline me for making.

The author of the New Testament book of Hebrews warns about "Not forsaking the assembling of ourselves together, as the manner of some is; but exhorting one another: and so much the more, as you see the day approaching" - Hebrews 10:25. This was a trap that I was slowly falling into in around year six or seven of my business. I was busy working all week and on Saturdays. Then on Sundays, I was working as an on-air personality at the radio station. What was omitted from my schedule was going to church. Now, I would catch a service here or there, but it was inconsistent and I was not faithfully attending prayer meetings. Now, I know you can pray at home in your prayer closet or even while you are driving in your truck. And you do not necessarily have to go to church to love God. In many cases, there are a lot of people who go to church that actually are not living in God's will. They may just be engaged in religion and tradition. But, in my case, I noticed in this season where my church attendance became inconsistent that my walk with the Lord was suffering. Where I once had a sharp discernment and an ever-growing hunger for God, now I was getting more caught up with the concerns of the world. My thoughts would be on who the Cleveland Browns play next or my mind was consumed with the pressing issues of my business. It was a slow decline, but the Lord was clearly not on the throne of my soul.

Again, let me clarify, that I do not exaggerate. I was still committed to living clean. I would still read my bible, pray, listen to worship music. But, in many ways, I felt like I was going through the motions. I felt like something was a little off. The Lord is jealous to be in the first place (the place of priority), and in my mind, will, and emotions He had competition.

The lesson I learned the hard way, is that I can not play games with God. He needs to be first in my life. First in my schedule, first in my business, first, in all I think, say, and do. In hindsight, I felt like in my business endeavors I was not always leaning on God's divine wisdom, strategy, and timing. Thankfully, He is kind and gave me a wake-up call and refreshed my passion to live for Him in a way that is fully pleasing. He is all about restoration.

I do have regret that I did not inquire of the Lord more in building my business. There were so many times I crashed and burned. So many poor decisions. Perhaps so much could have been avoided if I would have been more proactive in acknowledging God and asking for His help and guidance. The good news is His mercies are new every day. And each moment He allows me to be alive on this side of eternity, I want to love Him well.

Long story short I am currently back in the rhythm of consistently attending church on Sundays. There was a sacrifice I had to make to make this happen. I resigned from the on-air shift I did at the radio station on Sundays to create the time and space to go to church. Also, I set better boundaries with my schedule so that throughout the week I can attend the Wednesday night service and some of the prayer meetings. And once again I feel my heart is coming alive. Hope and peace fill my soul. There is also more of an awareness of how desperately I need God. I do not just need Him for salvation, healing, and deliverance. But, I need and want Him to lead and guide my business decisions. His perspective is so much higher and better than mine. And I want to take the time to seek the Lord and hear from Him on how to navigate my businesses. Not my will, but God's will be done.

My lawn care business was birthed out of a prayer, from that prayer walk back in the spring of 2011 when I desperately cried out to God for provision. My podcast and media company was birthed out of a vision I had while driving through rural Illinois. The Lord was front and center at the start of my business endeavors, but unfortunately, I so easily got distracted. Whether it was the busyness of a full schedule or even blinded by some success, the Lord has His ways of humbling us. And I am thankful for His kindness, but pray and plan in the future that I can keep Him first at all times. In the good times, on the bright days and also in the trying times and rainy days. I am learning to keep God in the first position and diligently and carefully obey His commandments.

25

PURSUING SUBSTANTIAL PROFIT MARGINS

My cousin Ryan once told me, "A smart man learns from his mistakes, but a wise man learns from the mistakes of others." Throughout the pages of this book I have shared many of the missteps I made in building my business. I want to reiterate the valuable lessons I learned about profits throughout the journey.

Being profitable is rewarding. Yet, achieving hefty profit margins can be very challenging when growing a lawn care and landscaping business. In the early phases of my business I was typically operating at a net loss. Eventually, after raising my prices and increasing efficiency, I was in the black. After improving the quality of our work, hiring a good bookkeeper, gaining more knowledge, and being intentional over the most microscopic details, I was able to enter into even more abundant profit margins.

Mike Michalowicz's book "Profit First" is a must-read for small business owners. I actually read it twice and teamed up with Gulf Coast Bookkeeping who uses Mike's system. Michalowicz so elegantly shared how as entrepreneurs we strut and show off the top line revenue. But, what is most important is the bottom line.

There are so many variables that affect the bottom line. In many ways our businesses are like the human body. There are so many intricacies with our bodies and how the various body parts affect one another. This became very real recently when I had an issue with my appendix. Thankfully, I was able to fully recover, but I painfully learned how one little body part can affect my overall health. But, what affects the health of our business, specifically the quest for substantial profit margins?

One of the key components is price. This was previously mentioned in the book and I repeat this point to emphasize how crucial it is that our prices are accurate in order that we experience the highest profit margins possible. So many are undercharging and leaving money on the table. Others are lazy and have not done the proper research of their market, the actual cost of their overhead and labor. I suggest doing the due diligence to really explore what the market is paying for the same services in your area. We need to gather as much detailed information so we can understand the market. And of course, we need to do a deep dive into the exact time each service will take to complete. For lawn maintenance, I recommend clocking in when you arrive at the property then clocking out when driving off. Do this for an entire season and then you will know what the average time per service is. That will help you know what to charge for that specific property and future properties of the same size. For design and build jobs I also recommend clocking in/out. Over time this data will give us more clarity of how long certain jobs take. That information will be helpful when compiling future bids. Since labor is the key variable in our pricing, we want to be meticulous in understanding how much time each service takes. Careful calculations are important so we can be earning the rate per man hour that makes us as profitable as possible.

A good price is only one small piece of the pie. There are several other important components to experience great profitability. Trimming those expenses is necessary for success. Depending on your specific niche, the operational expenses may vary, but no matter what they are we need to stay diligent making sure we are operating as lean and mean as possible. Shopping around and comparing different prices on expenses such as general liability and commercial vehicle insurance is just an example. We need to use the competitive markets to our advantage and make sure we are not wasting money overpaying for services or even worse paying for expenses that are not needed. One of my favorite hours of the month is my monthly profit meeting with Gulf Coast Bookkeeping. This is the meeting where we dive into the numbers and analyze how the business performed the previous month. This evaluation is significant in deciding what expenses can be cut or adjusted.

Another important component is efficiency. How much window time are we wasting with our team just enjoying the cruise around town? Having tight routes and great organization will help make sure when we are paying our employees for labor, that they are actually performing billable work. If we are paying our employees for 40 hours a week, then we should make sure they are in the field serving our customers those 40 hours.

Wasted time will diminish our profit margins. Many companies lose time in the morning, at those dreaded gas station trips, and on unwise commutes. In addition to efficiency with employees, it's essential that our equipment and software is as productive as possible. Utilizing the best tools to be as efficient as possible is a major key to enjoying the biggest profits.

Exceeding expectations is another ingredient to boost those profit margins. This is with the understanding that the other components to a strong foundation are in place. Our prices are bringing in the proper man hour rate, our efficiency is tight as possible, our expenses are as compact as possible, etc... When all those important infrastructures are in place and then we pursue excellence, quality work, the sky's the limit. Companies that do the highest quality work are able to charge premium pricing. Customers are willing to pay a little extra for outstanding work. It can be a temptation to slip in the quality of our work while trying to put out the other fires in our business. That is why it is so important we do things right and build the proper foundation, so we can give our best attention to wowing our customers with our matchless work.

26

SEPARATE YOURSELF FROM THE ORDINARY

A unique blend of circumstances has taught me to make every minute count. I hope the stories and strategies shared in this book have inspired and educated you no matter where you are on your entrepreneurial journey. Listening to podcasts and audiobooks while I am out working has been a game changer. Top tier athletes will go to the extreme to gain an edge above their competition. In business, we also must be intentional to stand out. With our busy lifestyles, listening to audiobooks and podcasts can be a great way to gain knowledge even while we are doing something else like driving or working.

Thankfully, there is a podcast that can help you learn from the best. The Green Industry Podcast is a show where we chat with industry executives, leaders, and trendsetters. The straightforward episodes are designed for those looking to take their businesses to the next level. You'll just have to experience it for yourself.

Our free podcast is available on all major podcast platforms.

In the event that you are looking for training and resources to get those sizzling sales and generate more profits check out www.greenindustrypodcast.com. Our world class website is full of solutions on how to get from where you are to where you want to be. If you are looking for expert solutions for your business we would love to help you change your life for the better.

ACKNOWLEDGEMENTS

I would like to acknowledge the best producer in the business, Mr. Producer. Most know Mr. Producer for his humor and incredible spirit of excellence behind his broadcast engineering. Not only does he produce my podcast, the Green Industry Podcast, but he also works for others in the industry such as Brian Fullerton, Keith Kalfas, Naylor Taliaferro, as well as many others such as athletes and influencers. Despite his full schedule, I am deeply appreciative to Mr. Producer for the ample amount of time and energy he invested into helping me create this book and for the production of the audiobook version. His attention to detail and high quality work is greatly appreciated. Mr. Producer, thank you my friend! If you ever are in need of audio production services, podcast editing or professional voice-over services, please send him a DM (Direct Message) on Instagram @mrproducerusa or contact us through the Green Industry Podcast website. He's not cheap but he is the "Best in the Biz."

Additionally, I would like to thank Beverly Mayer, Dr. Frank Holloman, and Bryan Race for your helpful input. I am grateful for your friendships and the huge encouragement you have been to me throughout this entire book creation process. Thank you!

Last, but not least, thank you to Brian and Liz Fullerton for your friendship and unimaginable generous support throughout my entrepreneurial journey. Your inspiration helped fuel me to complete this project.

Made in United States
Orlando, FL
19 October 2023

38025871R00085